how2become

GCSE French Is Easy

www.How2B_____.com

As part of this product you have also received FREE access to online tests that will help you to pass GCSE French Is Easy

To gain access, simply go to:

www.PsychometricTestsOnline.co.uk

Get more products
for passing any test at:

www.how2become.com

Orders: Please contact How2become Ltd, Suite 14, 50 Churchill Square Business Centre, Kings Hill, Kent ME19 4YU.

You can order through Amazon.co.uk under ISBN 978-1-910602-84-3, via the website www.How2Become.com or through Gardners.com.

ISBN: 978-1-910602-84-3

First published in 2016 by How2become Ltd.

Typeset for How2become Ltd by Anton Pshinka.

Disclaimer

Every effort has been made to ensure that the information contained within this guide is accurate at the time of publication. How2become Ltd are not responsible for anyone failing any part of any selection process as a result of the information contained within this guide. How2become Ltd and their authors cannot accept any responsibility for any errors or omissions within this guide, however caused. No responsibility for loss or damage occasioned by any person acting, or refraining from action, as a result of the material in this publication can be accepted by How2become Ltd.

The information within this guide does not represent the views of any third party service or organisation.

CONTENTS

INTRODUCTION TO YOUR GUIDE 7

VITAL VOCABULARY 11

SEASONS AND WEATHER 31

MY LIFE 35

LEISURE AND NEW MEDIA 57

HOME AND WIDER ENVIRONMENT 83

EDUCATION AND WORK 97

GRAMMAR 103

ANSWERS 129

INTRODUCTION
TO YOUR GUIDE

INTRODUCTION TO YOUR GUIDE

Hello, and welcome to your guide to GCSE French. Written by How2become, the UK's leading career specialists, this book will provide you with everything you need to revise GSCE French in as complete and concise a manner as possible.

GCSE French is Easy will become your go-to guide for all the information and advice you need for studying and passing GCSE French. Packed full of grammar resources, vocabulary lists, sample questions, and top tips, this revision guide will complement student's classroom learning and exam preparation.

GCSE French Examination

GCSE French is designed to test your understanding of the language, as well as your ability to use it in a variety of situations. No matter which exam board your school uses, you will need to have a command of essential verbs and vocabulary, and be extremely comfortable with core elements of grammar. Of course, this will be done through the study of specific modules, focusing on general topics such as 'the environment' or 'leisure activities'. In a nutshell, getting a good grade in GSCE French will require an ability to respond to and express many ideas and opinions, with accuracy.

As you know, you will have a reading exam, a listening exam, and a speaking exam, as well as controlled assessments to test your written communication in French.

So, being able to apply your knowledge of the module topics effectively, in a variety of mediums and contexts, is crucial for securing a high grade.

What the syllabus says

Undoubtedly, it would be extremely helpful to be aware of what the aims of the GCSE French course itself are. The government has set out specific objectives to include in the syllabus, in order to ensure teachers and exam boards are assessing particular skills and knowledge required to obtain a GCSE in French. By providing a detailed outline of the course, teachers and exam boards are able to tailor their resources to equip their students with basic French understanding; and ultimately add more focus and context to learning and revision.

Here are the key aims and outcomes of GSCE French according to the syllabus:

- *To enable students to communicate accurately, confidently, coherently, spontaneously and independently in French, with an enriched vocabulary in a fluent manner and variety of contexts.*

- *To enable students to understand clearly articulated French in standard speech, at near-normal speed, and to develop their ability and ambition to communicate with native speakers.*

- *To develop students' ability to respond to a range of (appropriately adapted) authentic French written material, including news articles and other literary texts.*

- *To encourage students to develop a wider cultural awareness and understanding of French identities and zeitgeists of societies. To have an ability to see beyond the common clichés in relation to French culture.*

The exams

So, finally, how will it all be examined? Of course, you know that four elements of your language course will be assessed via a listening, reading, speaking and written assessment. These four assessments are assessed and calculated and will count as part of your overall percentage grade.

Luckily, the major exam boards AQA, Edexcel and OCR all have a similar way of calculating the overall grade based on the four exams.

In a full French GCSE course from any of these exam boards, this is how you will be assessed:

Listening:

- You will be played extracts of French speech, which will be of varying speeds, lengths and difficulty, and will be both formal and informal.

- The questions, presented in English, are designed to test your ability in identifying, understanding, and responding to information.

- Answers are in French and English.

  (Examination result = 20% of your final grade)

Reading:

- You will be presented with text in a variety of forms (e.g. emails, newspapers, brochures), which will be of increasing complexity.

- Questions are given in English and will test how well you identify, understand, and respond to information.

- Answers are in French and English.

  (Examination result = 20% of your final grade)

Speaking:

- You will carry out two tasks (e.g. debate/discussion) that require you to interact with another speaker, who will most likely be your teacher.

- You will be marked on your use of French to present ideas and information, in multiple contexts and settings.

- It will also be marked by your teacher.

  (Controlled Assessment result = 30% of your final grade)

Writing:

- You will carry out two writing tasks on different subjects, in exam conditions at your school.

- You will be marked on your ability to convey ideas and points of view clearly, which are relevant to the task.

  (Controlled Assessment result = 30% of your final grade)

VITAL VOCABULARY

This chapter will deal with core vocabulary, phrases and verbs that are absolutely vital to understand and communicate French at any level.

Solid knowledge of this content will provide an excellent base for all further study, so although you will already be familiar with a lot of it, it can do no harm to remind yourself and practise these even further.

Being comfortable with numbers is vital at this level of French study, as many exam questions will incorporate them, and require the ability to understand and respond accurately using numbers.

WORKING WITH NUMBERS

1-30

Below are the first 30 numbers written for you in French. Make sure that you have a solid grasp of these numbers – these are very basic and you **WILL** be required to have a good knowledge regarding numbers.

> **TOP TIP!**
>
> You'll know these already, but make sure to note when hyphens are used and when they are not.

1	un	2	deux	3	trois	4	quatre
5	cinq	6	six	7	sept	8	huit
9	neuf	10	dix	11	onze	12	douze
13	treize	14	quatorze	15	quinze	16	seize
17	dix-sept	18	dix-huit	19	dix-neuf	20	vingt
21	vingt et un	22	vingt-deux	23	vingt-trois	24	vingt-quatre
25	vingt-cinq	26	vingt-six	27	vingt-sept	28	vingt-huit
29	vingt-neuf	30	trente				

40-100

Now that you have mastered the first 30 numbers in French, let's take a look at the numbers from 40 to 100.

TOP TIP!

Of course, numbers get more complicated as they get higher. Note when *vingt* takes an s and when it does not.

---

40 -	quarante	
50 -	cinquante	
60 -	soixante	
70 -	soixante-dix	*(literally 'sixty + ten')*
80 -	quatre-vingts	*(literally 'four twenties')*
90 -	quatre-vingt-dix	*(literally 'four twenties + ten')*
100 -	cent	

TEST YOURSELF!
- Write 'nineteen' in French: _____

- Write 'twenty-five' in French: _____

- Write 'quarante-quatre' in English: _____

- Write 'soixante-treize' in English: _____

- Write 'ninety-nine' in French: _____

100+

Beyond 100, numbers are nearly always formed using combinations of smaller numbers, although there are some new ones to learn.

TOP TIP!

You'll know these already, but make sure to note when hyphens are used and when they are not.

---

101 -	cent un	*(not 'cent et un')*
200 -	deux cents	
300 -	trois cents	
400 -	quatre cents	
500 -	cinq cents	
600 -	six cents	
700 -	sept cents	
800 -	huit cents	
900 -	neuf cents	
1.000 - (1,000)	mille	
2.000 - (2,000)	deux mille	
1.000.000 - (1,000,000)	un million	
2.000.000 - (2,000,000)	deux millions	
1.000.000.000 - (1,000,000,000)	un milliard	
2.000.000.000 - (2,000,000,000)	deux milliards	

TEST YOURSELF!

- Write 'one hundred and one' in French:

  _____

- Write 'three hundred and fourteen' in French:

  _____

- Write 'huit cent quatre-vingt-dix' in English:

  _____

- Write 'trois cent dix mille sept cent soixante-douze' in English:

  _____

- Write 'one million six hundred thousand two hundred and twelve' in French:

  _____

Common ways you'll have to deal with numbers

So, you've learnt what the numbers themselves are, but how will this knowledge be tested? You will need to become adept at recognising when numbers are being discussed, and familiarise yourself with useful common phrases.

Putting things in order

These are pretty straightforward, but be careful using *premier/première* – this changes when used before something that is masculine/feminine.

NUMBER	FRENCH SPELLING	FRENCH ABBREVIATION
First	premier/première	1er /1ere
Second	deuxième	2eme
Third	troisième	3eme
Fourth	quatrième	4ème
Fifth	cinquième	5ème
Sixth	sixième	6ème
Seventh	septième	7ème
Eighth	huitième	8ème
Ninth	neuvième	9ème
Tenth	dixième	10ème

Describing groups / approximates of numbers

Note that these sayings are all **feminine**.

There are about ten (...)	Il y a une dizaine (…)
There are about a dozen (...)	Il y a une douzaine (…)
There are dozens (...)	Il y a des douzaines (…)
There are about a hundred (...)	Il y a une centaine (…)
There are hundreds (...)	Il y a des centaines (…)
There are thousands (...)	Il y a des milliers (…)

TELLING THE TIME

Being able to tell the time will be a crucial part of your GCSE French exam. Take a look at the below phrases and see how they translate from French to English.

Asking and responding

Quelle heure est-il ?	What time is it?
Il est neuf heures	It is nine o'clock (a.m.)
Il est midi	It is midday
Il est minuit	It is midnight
Il est midi et demi	It is half past twelve (p.m.)
Il est quinze heures dix	It is ten past three (p.m.)
Il est vingt-trois heures et demie	It is half past eleven (p.m.)
À quelle heure est la reunion ?	What time is the meeting?
Elle est à treize heures pile	It's at 1pm sharp

Note how in French, a space is left between the question itself and the question mark! The same thing is done for other forms of punctuation, including exclamation marks, and various symbols such as the percentage symbol, and the Euro sign.

TOP TIP!

Generally, the French tell the time using the 24 hour clock, so, saying '6:45pm' is:

Dix-huit heures quarante-cinq

Dix heures
moins le quart

Sept heures
moins cinq

Huit heures dix

TOP TIP!

Expressions like 'quarter to', 'quarter past' and 'ten to' are still used, but only with the 12 hour clock – so be careful!

TEST YOURSELF!

Translate the following sentences:

- 'I have an appointment at 4pm.'

  _____

- 'I am going to the cinema at midday.'

  _____

- 'Je me lève à sept heures et quart tous les jours.'

  _____

- 'À quelle heure veux-tu sortir ? Vingt heures trente ?'

  _____

- 'I am going to visit my grandmother at quarter to seven tomorrow evening.'

  _____

Times of day

Le lever du soleil	Le petit matin	Le matin	L'après-midi
Sunrise	*The early hours*	*Morning*	*The afternoon*

Le soir	La nuit	Une heure tardive	Le soleil couchant
The evening	*Night*	*Late at night*	*Sunset*

PRACTICE EXAM QUESTIONS

My timetable

Three British students describe their school timetables. Read their conversation and then answer the questions below, **in English.**

Ashley : Moi, je dois arriver au collège à huit heures quarante pour être présent pour l'appel. Après, j'ai mon cours de français, qui se termine à dix heures.

Katie : A mon école, les classes commencent à neuf heures, et finissent pour le déjeuner à treize heures trente. Le reste de l'après-midi se passe avec plus d'études. On peut rentrer à la maison à quinze heures.

Stephen : Ma matière préférée, c'est la biologie. Il est le premier cours du matin, donc pour éviter d'arriver en retard, je quitte la maison à sept heures tous les jours. C'est important d'être à l'heure !

Question 1

At what time must Ashley arrive at school?

Question 2

What time does Katie's school break for lunch?

Question 3

What time does Stephen leave the house?

Question 4

Whose first lesson ends at 10?

Question 5

Who doesn't like being late?

Question 6

Who gets to go home at 3pm?

(Answers are provided at the end of the book).

CALENDARS AND DATES

Knowing what the days of the week and months are in French is vital, as is your ability to recognise and express them. This is something that will definitely be tested in your GCSE.

Days of the week

You will probably know these already, just be sure to note that the first letters of the days of the week are NOT capitalised, unlike English – unless they are at the start of a sentence.

Monday	Tuesday	Wednesday	Thursday	Friday	Saturday	Sunday
lundi	mardi	mercredi	jeudi	vendredi	samedi	dimanche

The weekend	Last Monday	Next Tuesday	On Wednesdays	Every/each Thursday
Le week-end	lundi dernier	mardi prochain	Le mercredi	Tous les jeudis/chaque jeudi

Today	Yester-day	Tomorrow	The following day	Every day / each day	In a week's time	A week ago
Aujourd'hui	Hier	Demain	Le lendemain	Tous les jours / chaque jour	Dans une semaine	Il y a une semaine

TEST YOURSELF!

Translate the following statements:

- 'Le vendredi, je fais du karaté au centre sportif.'

  _____

- 'Hier, j'ai vu la Joconde pour la première fois.'

  _____

- 'Je donne de l'argent aux sans-abri régulièrement, chaque weekend si possible.'

  _____

- 'My friend lost his phone in town last Wednesday.'

  _____

- 'Today is Sunday, and I am going to cook a big breakfast like I did last week.'

  _____

Months of the year

You will be familiar with these already, and they are all very similar to their English equivalents – just remind yourself which ones contain accents, and where.

janvier	février	mars	avril
mai	juin	juillet	août
septembre	octobre	novembre	décembre

Jour de l'An	New Year's Day
Pâques	Easter
La Fête du Muguet/La Fête du Travail (1er mai)	May Day
Fête de la Victoire (8 mai)	WW2 Victory Day
La Fête Nationale française (14 juillet)	Bastille Day
La Toussaint	All Saint's Day
Noël	Christmas
Saint-Sylvestre	New Year's Eve

Ce mois-ci – *this month*
Le mois dernier – *last month*
Le mois prochain – *next month*
En janvier dernier – *last January*

En février prochain – *next February*
Début mars – *at the beginning of March*
Fin avril – *at the end of April*
Le premier mai – *the first of May*

Quelle est la date aujourd'hui ?

What is the date today?

À quelle date...?

On what date...?

TEST YOURSELF!

Translate:
- 'My birthday is the 12th August'

  _____

- 'Le 19 mars est le premier jour du printemps'

  _____

- 'July 14th, Bastille Day, is a national holiday in France'

  _____

- 'À quelle date allez-vous au Siège des Nations Unies ?'

  _____

PRACTICE EXAM QUESTION

Planning a party

Read the following email from a friend, and answer the multiple choice questions below by giving **A, B or C.**

Salut,

Je t'envoie cet email parce qu'il faut organiser le fête pour l'anniversaire de Damien !

A mon avis, une date idéale serait près du début septembre, avant la fin des vacances d'été. Qu'est-ce tu dirais du premier samedi du mois ? L'année dernière, sa fête a eu lieu le quatorze septembre, et tous les invités étaient de mauvaise humeur, parce qu'ils devaient aller au collège le lendemain !

On doit embaucher un DJ – combien d'argent devrions nous dépenser ? Bien sûr, la musique est importante, mais il ne faut pas oublier les autres choses comme les amuse-gueules et des décorations qu'on pourrait vouloir. On peut en parler.

Aussi, dans une semaine, je vais rendre visite à la sœur de Damien pour demander son opinion. Veux-tu m'accompagner le soir du dix-huit ? Chez elle, on peut finaliser nos plans. Je n'ai qu'un but – une soirée géniale !

Bisous,

Laetitia

Question 1

Laetitia thinks that the party should be held...

    a. At the start of September

    b. In the middle of September

    c. At the end of September

Question 2

Why would Laetitia prefer this time of year?

    a. The weather will be nice

    b. There is a national holiday

    c. It will still be during the summer holiday

Question 3

On what date was Damien's last party?

    a. 14th September

    b. 13th September

    c. 20th September

Question 4

Why were the guests at Damien's last party in bad spirits?

    a. His parents were too strict

    b. The DJ was shocking

    c. They had school the next day

```
┌─────────────────────────────────────────┐
│                                         │
│                                         │
│                                         │
└─────────────────────────────────────────┘
```

Question 5

When does Laetitia plan to visit Damien's sister?

    a. The morning of the 19th

    b. The evening of the 18th

    c. At noon on the 12th

```
┌─────────────────────────────────────────┐
│                                         │
│                                         │
│                                         │
└─────────────────────────────────────────┘
```

SEASONS AND WEATHER

Learning the seasons is pretty straightforward, just be aware that they are all masculine.

Le printemps *spring*	**L'été** *summer*	**L'automne** *autumn*	**l'hiver** *winter*

Below I have listed some of the common types of weather. I have left additional space for you to practice using these words in a sentence.

Il pleut –	*it's raining*	
Il neige –	*it's snowing*	
Il fait beau –	*the weather is nice*	
Il fait chaud –	*it's hot*	
Il fait froid –	*it's cold*	
Il fait nuageux –	*it's cloudy*	
Il y a du soleil –	*it's sunny*	
Il y a du vent –	*it's windy*	

Il y a du brouillard –	*it's foggy*	
Il y a du tonnerre –	*there's thunder*	
Il y a des éclairs –	*there's lightning*	
Il y a de l'orage –	*it's stormy*	
Il y a de la grêle –	*it's hailing*	
Il y a de la brume –	*it's misty*	

WEATHER WARNINGS!

Ouragan	**Tsunami**	**Inondation**	**Tempête de neige**	**Foudre**	**Grêlon**
hurricane	*tsunami*	*flood*	*snowstorm*	*lightning bolt*	*hailstone*

MY LIFE

Now that the more basic stuff is out of the way, we are now going to move on to slightly harder French words and phrases.

Refer to this chapter as a reminder of how to correctly present yourself (useful for the speaking exam), describe your relationships with your family, express your hopes for the future, and go into detail about your daily routine, including discussing the theme of 'healthy living' more generally.

These topics are directly mentioned in the syllabus and will definitely crop up in an exam, so revise thoroughly!

DESCRIBING YOURSELF

Learning how to introduce yourself would have been a staple of your French study from Year 7 or even before that, but of course, at GCSE level, you are going to need to develop a stronger vocabulary and learn more advanced expressions in order to impress examiners.

Let's start with the basics, though:

Je me présente	*Let me introduce myself*
Je suis/je m'appelle	*I am/my name is*
J'ai…ans	*I am…years old*
Je suis au collège/lycée	*I am at school*
Je suis étudiant(e)	*I am a student*
J'habite…	*I live…*
Je m'intéresse à …	*I am interested in…*
J'aime m'habiller…	*I like to dress…*

SAMPLE SPEAKING EXAM

Présente-toi !

FRENCH

Je me présente. Je m'appelle Paul et j'ai seize ans. Mon anniversaire est en automne, le 21 septembre. Je suis étudiant du Lycée Jules-Ferry, qui se situe dans le 9ème arrondissement de Paris. J'habite près du lycée, dans un appartement avec ma famille. Je suis très sportif, et en plus **je m'intéressais toujours** au milieu de la mode. Donc, j'aime porter les vêtements de marque tous les jours.

Quant à ma personnalité, **je me considère prévenant et gentil**. Aussi, mes proches diraient que je suis extraverti, parce que j'adore sortir avec mes amis. **Cependant**, ma petite amie, Gabrielle, pense que je suis trop bavard ! Sinon, je suis assez travailleur et je prends au sérieux mes études, même si c'est possible que je passe trop de temps au gymnase. Pendant les vacances scolaires et le week-end, **j'y suis** tout le temps !

Note the variety of verb tenses and grammatical structures, relevant vocabulary, and expressing opinions! Of course, showing you can use a variety of constructions and elements of grammar will maximise your marks!

Je m'intéressais toujours – **Imperfect tense**

Je me considère - **Opinions**

Prévenant et gentil – **Relevant vocabulary/Adjectives**

Cependant – **Adverb**

J'y suis – **Pronoun**

Introduce yourself!

ENGLISH

Let me introduce myself. My name is Paul and I'm sixteen years old. My birthday is in autumn, on the 21st of September. I'm a student at Jules-Ferry Secondary School, which is located in the 9th arrondissement in Paris. I live close to the school, in a flat with my family. I am very sporty, and I have also always been interested in fashion. So, I like to wear branded clothing every day.

As for my personality, I consider myself as someone who's thoughtful and friendly. Also, those close to me would say that I am extroverted, because I love going out with my friends. However, my girlfriend, Gabrielle, thinks that I talk too much! Other than that, I'm quite hardworking and I take my studies seriously, even if I might spend too much time in the gym. During school holidays and weekends, I live there!

FAMILY AND RELATIONSHIPS

Questions surrounding family situations and relationships invariably come up in exams, and vocabulary surrounding this topic is of course helpful for real-word application. See below for key words presented in a family tree.

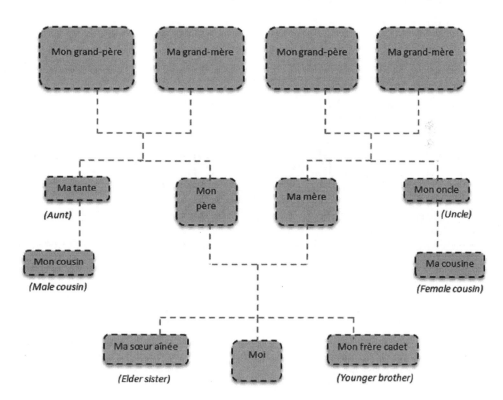

<u>More Vocabulary</u>

Le ménage/Le foyer – *household*

Une famille monoparentale – *a single parent household*

Le fils – *son*

La fille – *daughter*

Un enfant unique – *An only child*

L'ami(e) – *friend/boyfriend/girlfriend*

Le copain/la copine – *friend/boyfriend/girlfriend*

TOP TIP!

Consider context when working out which translation would be appropriate!

Le père/la mère célibataire – *single father/mother*

Le beau-père – *stepfather*

La belle-mère – *stepmother*

Le demi-frère – *half/stepbrother*

La demi-sœur – *half/stepbrother*

Describing Family Relationships

LES BONS	LES MAUVAIS
J'ai un bon rapport avec... *I have a good relationship with...*	**J'ai un rapport difficile avec...** *I have a difficult relationship with...*
Une relation stable : *A stable relationship*	**Être fâché(e) avec quelqu'un** *To be on bad terms with someone*
Je me sens soutenu(e) : *I feel supported*	**Ils me grondent trop** *They scold me too much*
Je fais confiance à... : *I trust...*	**Nous nous disputons souvent** *We often argue*
Attentif/Attentive aux mes besoins : *Attentive to my needs*	**Un manque de compréhension** *A lack of understanding*
Je m'entends bien avec... *I get on well with...*	**Il/Elle se moque de moi** *He/She mocks me*
Nous avons les mêmes centres d'intérêt : *We share the same interests*	**Un conflit de personnalité** *A personality clash*
On s'amuse bien ensemble : *We have fun together*	**Le comportement énervant** *Irritating behaviour*

PRACTICE EXAM QUESTION

My family life

Read the conversation between these students who are discussing their home lives. Answer the questions below **in English**.

Gigi : Je déteste ma vie familiale ! Je suis un enfant unique, et je ne l'aime pas du tout. Parce que je n'ai pas de frères ni de sœurs, mes parents me surprotègent. Nous nous disputons souvent, parce que je n'ai pas d'autonomie, et ils sont trop sévères. Par exemple, la semaine dernière, je n'ai pas eu le droit de sortir à une fête avec mes amies, car il y avait des garçons présents ! Quel manque de compréhension. Si je pouvais, je partirais !

Loïc : En général, je suis content à la maison. Je partage mon domicile avec mon père et mes deux sœurs aînées. J'ai un bon rapport avec tout le monde, et je me sens soutenu dans de nombreux aspects de ma vie – mon père est très marrant et il est mon modèle. Aussi, j'ai beaucoup des mêmes centres d'intérêts que mes sœurs. Si j'ai un reproche à faire ? Je ne suis pas toujours le centre d'attention !

Maurice : Je suis l'aîné de quatre enfants dans ma famille ; j'ai dix-sept ans et mon frère cadet, qui est casse-pieds, a trois ans. Je devais assumer beaucoup des responsabilités domestiques du foyer pour aider ma mère célibataire, par exemple je prépare les repas et je fais les courses. Je ne mets jamais en question la situation parce que ma mère a besoin d'aide, c'est aussi simple que ça. En plus, nous sommes fâchés avec notre père.

Adèle : Pour moi, la vie familiale a des hauts et des bas. J'habite avec ma mère, mon beau-père et son fils – mon demi-frère, qui est calme. Le nouveau ménage a été formé après la séparation de mes parents, et au début, j'étais malheureuse. Malgré l'effort de mon beau-père pour créer des liens entre nous, je le percevais comme un intrus. Mais, maintenant, nous nous entendons très bien.

Question 1

What two reasons does Gigi give for the frequent arguments with her parents?

Question 2

How many members of his family is Loïc on good terms with?

Question 3

How many older brothers does Maurice have?

Question 4

How did Adèle feel about her newly formed family situation at the start?

Question 5

Why wasn't Gigi allowed to go to the party?

Question 6

Loïc describes his father as being his role model, and shares many interests with his sisters, but what complaint does he give?

Question 7

What reason does Maurice give explaining why he never questions his responsibilities?

Question 8

How did Adèle initially perceive her stepfather, despite his efforts to bond with her?

(Answers are provided at the end of the book).

Relationships and Hopes for the Future

You may think that talking about relationships is an odd choice of topic for a GCSE syllabus, but as you probably know, discussing hopes and plans for the future is a common subject to come up in an oral exam situation.

Mon copain/Ma copine ideal(e)… *My ideal boyfriend/girlfriend…*	**Pour moi, un(e) mauvais(e) partenaire…** *For me, a bad partner…*
me rendait heureux/heureuse *would make me happy*	**me rendrait anxieux/anxieuse** *would make me anxious*
me donnerait du soutien *would give me support*	**serait trop égoïste** *would be too selfish*
serait fidèle *would be loyal*	**passerait trop de temps sur les réseaux sociaux** *would spend too much time on social media*
aurait sa propre indépendance *would have their own independence*	**serait paresseux/paresseuse** *would be lazy*
devrait avoir un bon sens de l'humeur *should have a good sense of humour*	**aurait des attitudes immatures** *would have immature attitudes*
serait romantique *would be romantic*	**ne me donnerait pas l'impression d'être spécial(e)** *wouldn't make me feel special*

Plans for the future:

- **Je n'ai pas l'intention de me marier**

  I do not intend to marry

- **Je n'ai aucun désir de m'installer !**

  I have no desire to settle down!

- **J'espère tomber amoureux/amoureuse**

  I hope to fall in love

- **Je voudrais fonder une famille à l'avenir**

  I would like to start a family in the future

- **Je n'y ai pas pensé – ma priorité actuelle est d'être accepté(e) à l'université**

  I have not thought about it – at the moment my priority is getting into university

KEY WORDS AND PHRASES

Rester célibataire – *Staying single*

Le mariage - *Marriage*

Le mariage civil – *Civil marriage*

Le mariage homosexual – *Same-sex marriage*

Le pacte civil de solidarité (PACS) – *Civil partnership*

L'union libre – *Living together*

Les fiançailles - *Engagement*

DAILY ROUTINE

Another regular speaking exam scenario is a conversation surrounding daily routine. A common way this could manifest itself is in the form of the prompt: 'Describe a normal day'.

See below for a sample response and its translation, but without the verbs conjugated! In the French version, fill in the correct forms of the verbs given in the paragraphs below. Note that many of them are reflexive!

Use these verbs and place them in the correct gaps below. Remember to conjugate them!

Se réveiller	Se lever	Rester	Se doucher	Se brosser	S'habiller	Prendre
wake up	*to wash*	*to stay*	*to have a shower*	*to brush*	*to get dressed*	*to take*
Quitter	Aller	Arriver	Devoir	Avoir	Rentrer	Se détendre
to leave	*to go*	*to arrive*	*to have to*	*to have*	*to come or get to work*	*to relax*
Regarder	Faire	Nettoyer	Préparer	Se coucher	Naviguer	S'endormir
to watch	*to do*	*to clean*	*to prepare*	*to go to bed*	*to navig*	*to go to sleep*

Bonjour ! Je vais te décrire ce qui constitue une journée normale pour moi. Premièrement, je me _réveille_ tous les jours à sept heures, mais d'habitude je ne me _____ pas avant sept heures et demie, car j'aime _rester_ au lit. Puis, je me _lève_. Si je suis en retard, je me _nettoye_ les dents en même temps ! Apres, je m' _____ rapidement, souvent je porte un jean skinny et un pull. Vers huit heures, je _____ mon petit déjeuner et je prépare à _____ la maison pour _____ au collège.

La plupart du temps, j' _arrive_ à ma salle de classe un peu tôt, parce que je _____ être présent pour l'appel. En plus, mon prof n' _____ pas le sens de l'humour quand on est en retard !

Donc, après une journée scolaire ardue, je peux _____ chez moi à seize heures et profiter de mon temps libre. Habituellement, dès que je suis à la maison, j'allume la télévision et je me _____ un moment. Les sitcoms me plaisent, je pourrais les _____ pendant des heures. Cependant, je ne peux pas passer toute la soirée à paraisser. Je dois _____ mes tâches ménagères. Premièrement, c'est à moi de _____ le salon si c'est en désordre, et je range ma chambre tous les jours par habitude. Ensuite, je _____ le dîner pour ma famille – mais j'adore cela.

Enfin, je vais aller me _____ à vingt-deux heures. Pourtant, je _____ toujours sur Internet au lit. J'aime passer une heure environ sur Twitter et YouTube avant de m' _____!

TRANSLATION

Hello! I am going to describe to you what constitutes a normal day for me. Firstly, I wake up 7 o'clock each day, but normally I do not get up until half past seven, as I like staying in bed. Then, I shower. If I am late, I brush my teeth at the same time! Afterwards, I get dressed to leave the house in order to get to school.

The majority of the time, I arrive at my classroom slightly early, because I have to be present for registration. Also, my teacher does not have a sense of humour when it comes to lateness!

So, after a difficult school day, I can go home at 4pm and enjoy some free time. Usually, as soon as I get in the house, I turn the TV on and relax for a while. I enjoy sitcoms, and I could watch them for hours. However, I can't spend the whole evening being lazy. I must help around the house. Firstly, it's up to me to clean up the living room if it is messy, and I tidy my room everyday as habit. After, I prepare dinner for the family, but I love to do this.

Finally, I go to bed at 10pm. But, I always browse the internet in bed. I like spending about an hour on Twitter and YouTube before I fall asleep!

LIVING HEALTHILY

The topic of healthy living is a very important one, as there is a vast array of ways your knowledge could be tested by examiners. Questions surrounding diet, exercise and stress, as well as alcohol and drugs, may well appear in all four of your French exams, so make sure you have an extensive 'Living Healthily' vocabulary at your fingertips!

Garder la forme	*To keep in shape*
Mener une vie saine	*To lead a healthy life*
Le régime alimentaire	*Diet (everyday)*
Faire attention à son poids	*To watch one's weight*
Être bien portant(e)	*To be well*
Se sentir en forme	*To feel fit*

Avoir des kilos en trop	*To be overweight*
La vie sédentaire	*Sedentary lifestyle*
Les risques pour la santé	*Health hazards*
Néfaste pour la santé	*Bad for your health*
Nuisible à la santé	Bad for your health
Un style de vie malsain	*An unhealthy lifestyle*

Constructing sentences using the present participle like this is a great way to add a variety of verb forms to your writing/speaking.

Proving to examiners you can use many verb forms = many marks!

Je garde la forme...

I keep fit...

- **En faisant de l'exercice**

  By doing exercise

- **En mangeant assez de fruits et légumes**

  By eating enough fruit and vegetables

- **En dormant suffisamment**

  By getting enough sleep

- **En évitant de boire trop d'alcool**

  By avoiding drinking too much alcohol

- **En s'abstenant de consommer des drogues**

  By abstaining from doing drugs

- **En choisissant de ne pas fumer**

  By choosing to not smoke

Used in this case, 'en' followed by the present participle of a verb translates to 'by'.

"Je garde la forme en comptant les calories !"

"I keep in shape by counting calories!"

PRACTICE EXAM QUESTION

Grasse Bretagne

Read the following article about obesity in Britain and answer the questions below, in English.

Selon l'Organisation des Nations Unies pour l'alimentation et l'agriculture, le Royaume-Uni est le pays avec les plus hauts taux d'obésité de l'Europe de l'Ouest. Les statistiques officielles montrent que 24,9% de la population britannique est considérée comme 'obèse', et avertissent que ce chiffre pourrait augmenter jusqu'à 50 % d'ici à 2050.

Évidemment cela représente un problème sérieux, mais quelles sont les causes ? On peut blâmer nos styles de vie modernes, qui dépendent grandement des voitures, de l'Internet, et du fast-food. En effet, nos vies sont devenues de plus en plus sédentaires, et les risques pour la santé sont devenus de plus en plus omniprésents.

Donc, il est clair que comme nation, on doit repenser nos habitudes et évoluer vers une société plus active, plus responsable, plus saine et plus contente. Nous ne pouvons pas continuer sur cette voie d'irresponsabilité.

Mais comment y parvenir ? Ce qui est nécessaire est une approche à deux volets : des mesures pratiques du côté gouvernemental, et des actions personnelles. Tout d'abord, le gouvernement doit sévir contre la consommation excessive d'alcool, et hausser les impôts sur le tabac – les maladies du foie et du poumon coûtent au NHS des millions de livres par an. De plus, pour encourager les jeunes à faire de l'exercice, il faut baisser les frais d'adhésion aux gymnases et aux clubs de sport.

En attendant, le grand public doit être proactif en choisissant de vivre sainement. Par exemple, il n'est pas trop difficile de manger plus de fruits et légumes, et le gain de poids peut être ralenti en dormant suffisamment et en gérant bien le stress.

En résumé, l'obésité est l'un des problèmes sanitaires les plus graves de nos jours, et pour y faire face, nous devons agir de manière décisive, de peur que nous nous condamnions à un désastre.

Question 1

What does the Food and Agriculture Organisation of the United Nations say about the UK? Give **one** point mentioned.

Question 2

According to the second paragraph, what **two** aspects of our modern lifestyles are to blame?

Question 3

According the third paragraph, what can we **not** do?

Question 4

Out of the three mentioned, name **two specific actions** the government should take, according to the fourth paragraph.

Question 5

Apart from eating more fruits and vegetables, what else is said to help slow down weight gain? Give the **two** points mentioned in the fifth paragraph.

Question 6

Summarise the message of the final paragraph.

(Answers are provided at the end of the book).

DRINKING AND DRUG USE

<u>French Drinking Customs!</u>

As you probably know, the French adhere to certain etiquette when drinking alcohol is involved. If you find yourself (of age) in France in a social situation, make sure you are aware of these. If you are not yet of age, simply say *"Non merci, je suis mineur."*

<u>Here are three main customs that most French people take very seriously!</u>

- If you are at a dinner party that is somewhat formal, only take your first sip when your host does – he or she will wait until everyone at the table has their drink in front of them.

- If you are just in a pub or bar, people will say '*à ta santé*' (to your health), to which you can reply '*à la tienne*' (and to yours). Of course, use '*à la vôtre*' if necessary!

- When you clink glasses with someone, you must make eye contact with them while doing so. It is considered bad luck if this does not happen, and therefore you could come across as rude if you don't remember this. It is also considered bad luck to clink glasses filled with drinks that aren't alcoholic!

La boisson alcoolisée	Alcoholic drink
Prendre quelques verres entre amis	Having a few drinks with friends
Se détendre	To unwind
Perdre ses inhibitions	To lose one's inhibitions
L'ivresse	Drunkenness
L'abus d'alcool	Alcohol abuse

Un stupéfiant	A drug
Les drogues douces	Soft drugs
Les drogues dures	Hard drugs
Une pente glissante	A slippery slope
Devenir accro	To become addicted
S'adonner à quelque chose	To become hooked on something
Un toxicomane	Drug addict
Le soutien gouvernemental	Government support
Le projet de réinsertion	Rehabilitation programme

À mon avis...

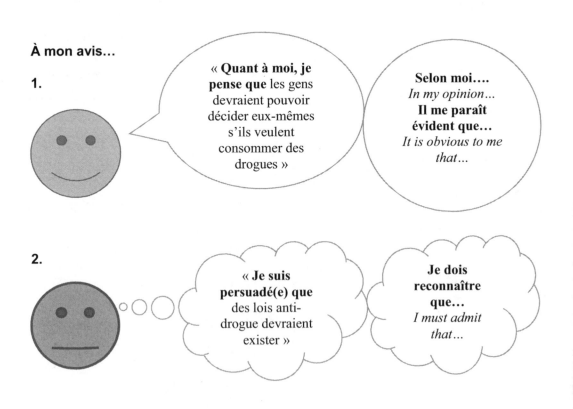

1.

« **Quant à moi, je pense que** les gens devraient pouvoir décider eux-mêmes s'ils veulent consommer des drogues »

Selon moi....
In my opinion...
Il me paraît évident que...
It is obvious to me that...

2.

« **Je suis persuadé(e) que** des lois anti-drogue devraient exister »

Je dois reconnaître que...
I must admit that...

3.

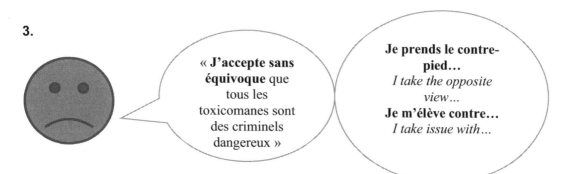

« **J'accepte sans équivoque** que tous les toxicomanes sont des criminels dangereux »

Je prends le contre-pied…
I take the opposite view…
Je m'élève contre…
I take issue with…

Note how inverted commas and speech marks are transcribed in French, using the jazzy arrows: « »

Match the above opinions to their correct translations below by writing 1, 2 or 3 in the corresponding boxes:

I accept unequivocally that all drug addicts are dangerous criminals.

In my opinion, people should be able to decide themselves if they want to take drugs

I'm certain that some anti-drug laws should exist

LEISURE
AND
NEW MEDIA

The next module topic is 'Leisure and New Media'. In this chapter, we will cover talking about free time in more detail, including going on holiday, as well as what the syllabus still calls 'new technology', i.e. the Internet and devices popular with young people. As you know, these subjects will potentially appear in all four of your assessments, so let's get started.

FREE TIME

Although we touched upon this topic when looking at daily routine, 'Free Time' deserves a section of its own, as examiners love making you talk about it in speaking and writing exams. So, having some phrases and vocab in your back pocket is very advisable.

En semaine	On weekdays
Le weekend	On weekends
Je suis très actif/active pendant mon temps libre	I am very active in my free time
Moi, je préfère me relaxer	Me, I prefer to relax
Mes goûts musicaux	My music tastes
Mon sport préféré	My favourite sport
Mes émissions favorites	My favourite programmes
Mes passe-temps/Mes loisirs	My hobbies
Se réunir entre copains	To get together with friends
Les jeux vidéo	Video games
Un cinéphile	A regular filmgoer
Visiter les musées	Visiting museums
Fréquenter les galeries d'art	Going to art galleries
Il y a un manque de distractions en ville	There is a lack of facilities /There's nothing to do in town
Les jeunes ne sont pas favorisés	Young people are not prioritised/ favoured

PRACTICE EXAM QUESTION

My hobbies

Read the conversation between these British students who are discussing what they like to do in their free time. Answer the questions below by circling either **TRUE, FALSE or NOT MENTIONED**.

Erik : Mon temps libre a toujours été occupé par le sport et la musique. Je suis membre d'une équipe de basket, et nous concourons au niveau national. Donc, je consacre beaucoup d'heures en semaine à l'entraînement, et la plupart du weekend se déroule aussi activement. En plus, la musique est très importante pour moi. Je l'utilise pour me déconnecter de ce monde, et me relaxer.

Harry : Je passe au moins deux heures par jour au skate-park dans ma ville. Je n'aime pas du tout le football - le skate, c'est ma passion. Mais, jusqu'à l'année dernière quand le skate-park a été construit, moi et mes potes n'avions nulle part où aller pour faire ce que nous aimons. Nous devions faire du skate dans la rue. Il va sans dire que les gens du coin étaient souvent en colère, mais maintenant tout va bien.

Gemma : Je m'intéresse fortement aux jeux vidéo, et je consacre une grande partie de mon temps libre à y jouer sur ma console. Mon genre préféré ? Ce sont les jeux de tirs ou de puzzle, mais j'essaierai à tout. Avec mon Xbox, je connecte à Internet pour me réunir avec mes amis. Nous avons la possibilité de parler ensemble, et bien sûr, de jouer ensemble. C'est chouette !

Daniel : Et moi, je suis un lecteur assidu. En dehors du lycée, je dévore un livre par semaine, typiquement je choisis un roman américain ou quelque chose d'Émile Zola. En revanche, je ne regarde jamais la télévision, ça ne sert à rien. Mais, j'aime visiter des musées et je passe chaque week-end dans une galerie d'art. M'immerger dans la haute culture, c'est ma vie.

Question 1

Erik uses basketball to switch off and relax.

TRUE	FALSE	NOT MENTIONED

Question 2

Skating is Harry's passion.

TRUE	FALSE	NOT MENTIONED

Question 3

Gemma hates gaming on PC.

TRUE	FALSE	NOT MENTIONED

Question 4

Daniel likes watching television.

TRUE	FALSE	NOT MENTIONED

Question 5

On weekdays, Erik spends many hours training.

TRUE	FALSE	NOT MENTIONED

Question 6

Harry started skating when the skatepark was built in his town.

TRUE	FALSE	NOT MENTIONED

Question 7

Videogames play a role in Gemma's social life.

TRUE	FALSE	NOT MENTIONED

Question 8

Daniel loves immersing himself in high culture.

TRUE	FALSE	NOT MENTIONED

(Answers are provided at the back of the book).

FASHION

This may seem like a niche topic, but it is a useful gateway into subjects such as youth culture and self-expression.

Relevantly and accurately discussing wider concepts like this in writing and speaking exams is guaranteed to boost your marks, as you may not have been specifically prompted to do so.

Showing examiners that you can take the initiative in this way is a great way to impress them, as long as doing so makes sense for the question!

Basic Vocab

Les vêtements - *Clothes*
Une chemise – *A shirt*
Un T-shirt – *A T-shirt*

Un jean – *(A pair of) Jeans*
Une jupe – *A skirt*
Un pantalon – *(A pair of) Trousers*

La coiffure	Hairstyle
Le maquillage	Makeup
Un tatouage	A tattoo
Le perçage/Le piercing	Piercings
Une robe	A dress
Un costume	A suit

Suivre la mode	To follow fashion
Les vêtements de marque	Designer clothes
Les marques les plus cotées	The most popular brands
À la mode	In fashion
La nouveauté	The newest trend

L'auto-expression	Self-expression
Un élément important de l'identité et de la culture des jeunes	An important part of youth identity and culture
J'aime me démarquer des adultes	I like to distinguish myself from the adults

SAMPLE SPEAKING EXAM

Comment dépenses-tu ton argent de poche ?

Je m'appelle Jules, et **je vais vous dire** comment je dépense mon argent de poche. Je reçois dix euros par semaine, en échange de tâches ménagères.

Personnellement, j'aime les achats de vêtements. Je suis fanatique de la mode, et je consacre une grande partie de mon argent à ajouter à ma collection de baskets, de bijoux, de chemises - tout et n'importe quoi. C'est important pour moi de me tenir au courant **des nouveautés.**

S'il est vrai que je préfère les vêtements de marque, je suis opposé à l'avis qu'une passion pour la mode équivaille à être superficiel. Pour moi, la mode représente une façon importante de m'exprimer, sans laquelle je perdrais mon identité.

Note the variety of verb tenses and grammatical structures, relevant vocabulary, and expressing opinions! Of course, showing you can use a variety of constructions and elements of grammar will maximise your marks!

Je vais vous dire – **Immediate future tense**

Personnellement – **Adverb**

Nouveautés – **Relevant vocab**

Translation:

How do you spend your pocket money?

My name is Jules, and I am going to tell you how I spend my pocket money. I get 10 euros per week, in exchange for doing some household chores.

Personally, I love clothes shopping. I am a fashion fanatic, and I devote a large amount of my money to adding to my collection of trainers, jewellery, shirts - anything and everything. It's important for me to keep up to date with the latest trends.

While it's true that I prefer branded clothing, I'm against the view that a passion for fashion equates to being superficial. For me, fashion represents an important way of expressing myself, without which I would lose my identity.

Here is some space for you to answer the question: "Quelle est l'importance de la mode dans ta vie ?" in the context of a speaking exam response.

TRAVEL

Being able to speak about forms of transport and tourism is very useful at any level, and some knowledge of vocabulary surrounding these subjects is almost guaranteed to be tested in at least one of your exams.

Of course, confidence in this regard will also be indispensable when you find yourself in a French-speaking country, as you will be better prepared for getting yourself around!

Basic Directions

Asking for basic directions can get very complicated. For example, 'How do I get to the train station?' is most accurately translated as *'Comment est-ce que je fais pour aller à la gare ?'*

However, it is also correct to use the much simpler: 'Where is the train station, please?' i.e. *'Où est la gare, s'il vous plaît ?'*

Basic responses to these types of questions, especially in exam scenarios, could include:

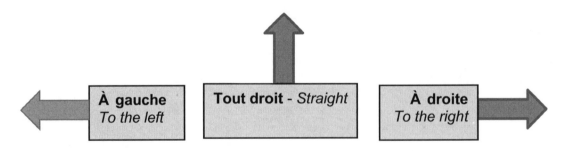

Au bout de la rue	*At the end of the street*
Au coin de la rue	*Around the corner*
À côté de...	*Next to...*
Aller/Prendre/Traverser/Suivre	*Go/Take/Cross/Follow*

Loin d'ici	Far from here
Près d'ici	Close by

Getting Around Locally

À pied – *On foot*

À vélo – *By bike*

En autobus – *By bus*

En train – *By train*

En voiture – *By car*

En taxi – *By taxi*

En métro – *By metro/underground*

En tram – *By tram*

Réseaux de transport – *Transport networks*

Efficace/Fiable – *Reliable*

Insuffisant - *Insufficient*

Travelling Abroad

Un trajet – *a trip*

Un séjour – *a stay*

Un voyage – *a journey*

Le transport aérien low-cost – *Budget air travel*

L'aéroport – *The airport*

À l'heure – *On time*

Retardé – *Delayed*

Annulé - *Cancelled*

Douane/Contrôle de passeport – *Customs/Passport control*

La porte – *Gate*

Holidays

Un vacancier – *A holidaymaker*

Une évasion – *An escape*

Les forfaits – *Package deals*

Faire du tourisme – *To go sightseeing*

Réserver un chambre d'hôtel – *To book a hotel room*

Une station balnéaire – *A beach resort*

Une croisière – *A cruise*

Une station de ski – *A ski resort*

Les vacances vertes – *A holiday in the country*

Les vacances actives – *An activity holiday*

Un court séjour dans une grande ville – *A city break*

Un second chez-soi – *A home away from home*

Pays Francophones	French-Speaking Countries
La France	France
La Côte d'Ivoire	Ivory Coast
Le Sénégal	Senagal
Le Cameroun	Cameroon
Madagascar	Madagascar
Le Canada	Canada
La Belgique	Belgium
Monaco	Monaco
La Suisse	Switzerland

Raisons de voyager

Pour se relaxer – *To relax*

Pour découvrir – *To discover*

Pour avoir du plaisir – *To have fun*

Pour faire une expérience authentique – *To have an authentic experience*

Vivre comme tout le monde – *To live like a local*

PRACTICE EXAM QUESTION

The evolution of tourism

Read the following article about emerging trends in the travel industry and answer the questions below, **in English**.

De nouveaux chiffres des sites de voyage indiquent que l'année dernière, les escapades citadines étaient aussi appréciées que les vacances sur la plage pour la première fois. La popularité de ce type de tourisme a augmenté dramatiquement chez les Britanniques au cours des dernières années, avec de plus en plus des courts séjours en Europe réservés chaque printemps, été, et automne.

Cette nouvelle tendance peut être expliquée par de nombreux facteurs. Premièrement, les Britanniques sont devenus plus aventureux dans le choix d'une destination touristique, abandonnant leurs « seconds chez soi » en Espagne pour découvrir des nouveaux pays.

De plus, il y a eu une croissance des compagnies aériennes low-cost, qui desservent une large gamme de destinations. Donc, les vacanciers ont commencé de profiter de cette opportunité. C'est la norme d'embarquer dans un avion pour un pays sur le continent, faire un tour d'Europe en train, et rentrer par un aéroport différent.

Finalement, les jeunes ont eu une influence notable. La véritable révolution de la culture smartphone a donné lieu au touriste hyperinformé - quelqu'un qui a toutes les informations sur le bout des doigts, littéralement. Cela a conduit à une intensification du tourisme vers des villes européennes considérées comme « non traditionnelles », tels que Tallinn en Estonie et Gdansk en Pologne.

Question 1

What does the first paragraph indicate about the popularity of city breaks compared to beach holidays these days?

Question 2

How have British tourists' behaviour changed according to paragraph 2?

Question 3

Summarise the information given in the third paragraph.

Question 4

According to paragraph 4, what has given rise to the hyper-informed tourist?

Question 5

Look at the first paragraph. How has the rise in popularity of city breaks manifested itself?

Question 6

Considering the article as a whole, what are the **three** specific reasons for the rise in popularity of city breaks?

(Answers are provided at the end of the book).

TV AND CINEMA

Although we have already covered 'Free Time', the topic of TV and Cinema could be the specific focus of your writing or speaking exam.

Specific vocabulary on this subject will most likely be required to successfully navigate the listening and reading exams.

L'Actualité/Les informations/ Les nouvelles	*The news*
La météo	*The weather forecast*
Un feuilleton	*A soap*
Un jeu télévisé/Une émission de jeux	*A gameshow*
Une sitcom	*A sitcom*
Un dessin animé	*A cartoon*
La télécommande/La zapette	*The remote control*
Devant l'écran	*In front of the screen*
Se gaver de séries sur Netflix	*To binge-watch a series on Netflix*

La Publicité

Une publicité/Une pub –

Un spot publicitaire – 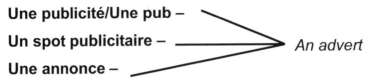 *An advert*

Une annonce –

Les spots TV sont agaçants – *TV adverts are annoying*

Ils sont partout/omniprésents – *They are everywhere*

Nous sommes bombardés – *We are bombarded*

Ils sont souvent sexistes - *They are often sexist*

Un mal nécessaire ? – *A necessary evil?*

<u>Un débat !</u>

> À mon avis, le gouvernement doit limiter le volume de publicité auquel nous sommes exposés, ce n'est pas juste !

> Moi, je ne vois pas où est le problème. Les annonces me donnent des informations utiles sur des bons produits.

> C'est une forme de contrôle inacceptable - perpétuée par de grandes sociétés avides de profit !

> Personne ne t'oblige à dépenser ton argent ! C'est une question de contrôle de soi.

Le Cinéma

Un film…

…d'action - *action*

…d'aventures - *adventure*

…de suspense - *thriller*

…à grand spectacle - *epic*

…d'horreur - *horror*

…comique - *comedy*

…d'animation - *animation*

…à gros succès – *blockbuster*

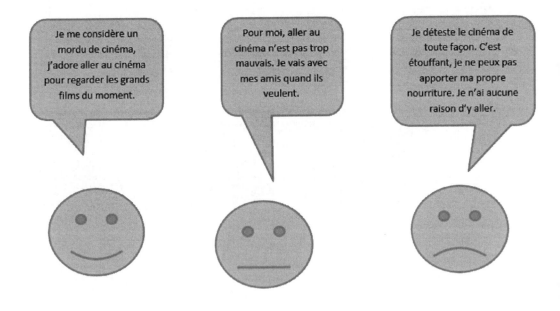

Je me considère un mordu de cinéma, j'adore aller au cinéma pour regarder les grands films du moment.

Pour moi, aller au cinéma n'est pas trop mauvais. Je vais avec mes amis quand ils veulent.

Je déteste le cinéma de toute façon. C'est étouffant, je ne peux pas apporter ma propre nourriture. Je n'ai aucune raison d'y aller.

THE INTERNET

'The Internet' is a topic that is going to appear in language exams in greater depth and with greater frequency as years go by. Of course, more and more Internet vocabulary is coming into practice every day, much of which causes debate in France over how to best translate it!

At GCSE level, exam questions about Internet habits and social media have become almost guaranteed, so make sure you know lots of specialist vocabulary.

Un internaute	*An Internet user*
Un ordinateur de bureau	*A desktop computer*
Un ordinateur portable	*A laptop*
Le clavier	*The keyboard*
La souris	*The mouse*
Une connexion Wifi	*A Wifi connection*
Un site Web/Un site Internet	*A website*
Un moteur de recherche	*A search engine*
Un navigateur	*A browser*
Une adresse email	*An email address*

Cliquer – *To click*

Un clic – *A click*

Copier-coller – *Copy and paste*

Un code d'accès – *Password*

Un lien – *A link*

Un smartphone	A smartphone
Une tablette	A tablet
Données mobiles	Mobile data
Navigation mobile	Mobile browsing
Une app/Une appli	An app

Le chargeur – *Phone charger*
La durée d'autonomie – *Battery life*

Télécharger de la musique	Downloading music
Le streaming	Streaming
Télécharger une vidéo sur YouTube	Uploading a video to YouTube

Un téléchargement - *A download*

Social Media

Médias sociaux – *Social media*

Poster sur Facebook – *To post on Facebook*

Demande d'amitié – *Friend request*

Le journal – *Timeline*

Photo de profil – *Profile picture*

Envoyer un tweet/Tweeter – *To tweet*

Un tweet – *A tweet*

Retweeter quelque chose – *To retweet something*

Envoyer un message direct – *Send a direct message*

Une story Snapchat - *A Snapchat story*

Une discussion de group – *A group chat*

Un groupe WhatsApp – *A WhatsApp group*

Aimer une photo sur Instagram – *Liking a photo on Instagram*

Un appel Skype – *A Skype call*

Below are some opinions about the benefits and risks of social media and smartphones, **match** the opinions in French to their correct translations by drawing lines, and learn the useful phrases and vocab! The first matches have been made to serve as examples.

Les bienfaits

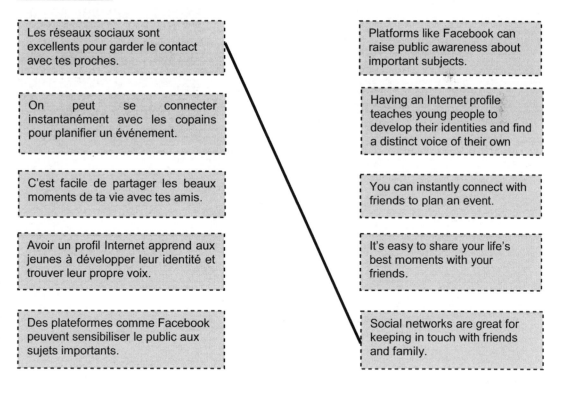

Les réseaux sociaux sont excellents pour garder le contact avec tes proches.

On peut se connecter instantanément avec les copains pour planifier un événement.

C'est facile de partager les beaux moments de ta vie avec tes amis.

Avoir un profil Internet apprend aux jeunes à développer leur identité et trouver leur propre voix.

Des plateformes comme Facebook peuvent sensibiliser le public aux sujets importants.

Platforms like Facebook can raise public awareness about important subjects.

Having an Internet profile teaches young people to develop their identities and find a distinct voice of their own

You can instantly connect with friends to plan an event.

It's easy to share your life's best moments with your friends.

Social networks are great for keeping in touch with friends and family.

Les risques

Il est possible de devenir accro aux médias sociaux, et on risque de perdre le lien avec le monde réel.

Certains défendent l'idée que l'obsession des smartphones a un effet néfaste sur la santé mentale.

Le partage à outrance des renseignements personnels en ligne peut mener à la fraude ou au vol.

Un comportement irresponsable sur un média social pourrait te coûter un emploi à l'avenir

L'exposition aux écrans brillants perturbe le sommeil.

There is an argument for the idea that an obsession with smartphones can have a damaging effect on mental health.

Exposure to bright screens disturbs sleep.

It is possible to become addicted to social media, and you can risk losing your connection to the real world.

Oversharing personal details online could lead to fraud or theft.

Irresponsible behaviour on a social media site could cost you a job in the future.

SAMPLE WRITING EXAM

Module: Technology

Task: In order to better understand her young constituents and their online lives, a member of your local council has asked you to write to her about young people and the Internet.

She would like you to give opinions on the use of social media in today's society, as well as discuss your own online presence and Internet habits.

Include details of the following:

1. How often you use various social media platforms

2. Your opinions on the benefits of social media

3. Your opinions on the 'dark side' of social media: oversharing, bullying

---

Chère conseillère,

Je vais vous donner mes impressions sur l'utilisation d'Internet par les jeunes, et discuter de leurs habitudes en ce qui concerne les médias sociaux.

Premièrement, il est indéniable que les vies sociales des jeunes de nos jours sont fortement liées aux plateformes en ligne telles que Facebook et Twitter. Des milliers de nouveaux utilisateurs s'inscrivent chaque jour à tous les types de ces réseaux, et les apps comme Instagram et Snapchat sont téléchargées des millions de fois par jour. Internet est devenu le moyen de communication le plus utilisé parmi les jeunes, et il représente un outil important pour s'exprimer.

Personnellement, je passe plusieurs heures sur mon portable tous les jours, naviguant sur mes journaux de Facebook et Twitter. J'aime bavarder avec mes amis et rechercher des mèmes Internet- parce que ça me fait rire. En plus, je suis constamment branché sur des services de messagerie comme WhatsApp, donc je reçois beaucoup d'alertes et de notifications au long de la journée. Jusqu'à récemment, cela m'empêchait

---

de travailler souvent, mais j'ai depuis appris qu'il est préférable d'éteindre le smartphone lorsqu'il faut étudier. Je ne suis plus si facilement distrait !

Oui, je dois admettre que je suis accro à mon smartphone, et mon expérience me montre qu'Internet représente une addiction pour la plupart des adolescents. Pourtant, je ne pense pas que ce soit nécessairement une mauvaise chose, parce que le développement d'Internet et la forte influence que la technologie exerce sur la vie moderne ne peuvent qu'être bénéfiques à long terme. Je vais expliquer – je suis certain que l'innovation technique dans un domaine comme la médicine va continuer de nous étonner à jamais.

De plus, on ne peut pas oublier les avantages évidents des médias sociaux, et comment ils aident les jeunes dans la vie quotidienne. Par exemple, la communication numérique est indispensable au développement des relations et des amitiés. Sans doute, ce serait très difficile pour un lycéen de s'intégrer à un cercle d'amis sans aucune forme de présence en ligne. De plus, je ne pense pas que cela montre la superficialité de la génération moderne, car ce n'est pas leur faute ils vivent à l'ère d'Internet.

Pourtant, je suis conscient qu'une connexion constante n'est pas sans inconvénient. Bien sûr, il y a un côté obscur aux médias sociaux. D'abord, on peut dire qu'une minorité de jeunes ne les utilisent pas de manière suffisamment responsable. Par exemple, le partage à outrance des renseignements personnels pourrait mettre en danger quelqu'un, et il est essentiel de savoir à qui on s'adresse à tout moment. Aussi, un défi de nos jours est la lutte contre le cyberintimidation et le harcèlement électronique, qui ont le potentiel de détruire des vies.

En conclusion, je suis convaincu que les éléments positifs d'Internet et des réseaux sociaux l'emportent sur les éléments négatifs. Je crois qu'avec une éducation sur la sécurité en ligne, on doit faire confiance aux jeunes les croire capables d'être responsables dans leur vie sur Internet, et leur donner la liberté de s'exprimer, de surfer, et de parler comme ils veulent, malgré les dangers potentiels.

Je vous prie d'agréer, chère conseillère, mes salutations distinguées.

Stan Tang

Note the variety of verb tenses and grammatical structures, relevant vocabulary, and expressing opinions!

ce qui– **Relative pronoun**

est devenu – **'Être' verb**

le moyen le plus utilisé – **Superlative**

cela m'empêchait – **Imperfect tense**

et/mais/lorsque – **Range of conjunctions**

je ne pense pas/il ne peut que/je ne suis plus – **Range of negative expressions**

je suis convaincu – **Passive voice, past participle**

Translation:

Dear Councilmember,

I am going to give you my impressions about how young people use the Internet, and discuss their habits surrounding social media.

Firstly, it is undeniable that in this day and age, young people's social lives are strongly linked to online platforms such as Facebook and Twitter. Thousands of new users sign up to all types of these networks every day, and apps like Instagram and Snapchat are downloaded millions of times per day. The Internet has become the most used method of communication amongst young people, and it represents an important tool of self-expression.

Personally, I spend several hours a day on my phone, browsing my Facebook and Twitter timelines. I love talking with my friends and searching for Internet memes, because it makes me laugh. Also, I am constantly connected to messaging services like WhatsApp, so I receive many alerts and notifications throughout the day.

Until recently, this often distracted me, but I have since learned that it's best to turn my smartphone off when it is time to work. I am no longer so easily distracted!

Yes, I must admit that I am addicted to my smartphone, and my experience tells me that the Internet represents an addictive force for most adolescents. However, I do not think that this is necessarily a bad thing, because the development of the Internet and the strong influence that technology holds in our modern lives can only benefit us in the long run. I will explain – I am certain that technical innovation in areas such as medicine will continue to amaze us forever.

Also, we cannot forget the obvious advantages of social media, and how it helps young people in daily life. For example, digital communication is indispensable in the development of relationships and friendships. Without a doubt, it would be very difficult for a secondary school student to integrate into a circle of friends without any form of online presence. What's more, I don't think that this shows the modern generation to be superficial, as it is not their fault that they live in the Internet age.

However, I am aware that being constantly connected is not without its disadvantages. Of course, there is a dark side to social media. Firstly, it is possible to say that a minority of young people do not use them with enough responsibility. For example, the oversharing of personal details could put someone in danger and it is essential to know who you are talking to at all times. Also, a challenge of today is the fight against cyberbullying and online harassment, which have the potential to destroy lives.

But, in conclusion, I am convinced that the positive elements of the Internet and social networks outweigh the negatives. I believe that with education about online safety, we should place our trust in young people to be responsible with their Internet lives, and give them the freedom to express themselves, surf, and talk how they want, despite the potential dangers.

Yours sincerely,

Stan Tang

HOME
AND WIDER
ENVIRONMENT

Similarly to the topic of the Internet, discussing the environment and your local area requires a fair amount of specific vocabulary.

However, this is a very ideal topic for proving that you can express ideas and opinions in French, so knowing a variety of phrases to do with introducing and justifying opinions will be invaluable in writing and speaking exams.

Let's start with some basic vocab:

Au nord-est	Au nord-ouest	Au sud-est	Au sud-ouest
In the north-east	*In the north-west*	*In the south-east*	*In the south-west*

Ma grande ville	*My city*
Ma ville	*My town*
Mon village	*My village*
Ma banlieue	*My suburb*
Mon voisinage	*My neighbourhood*
Ma région	*My area*
Ma cité	*My estate*
Un milieu urbain	*An urban area*

Une région rurale	A rural area
À la compagne	In the countryside
Dans une ferme	On a farm
Un centre commercial	A shopping centre
Les grands magasins	Department stores
Des cafés et restaurants	Cafés and restaurants
Des musées	Museums
Une bibliothèque	A library
Un cinéma	A cinema
Un centre de loisirs	Leisure centre

Landmarks

Une statue

Un monument

Une cathédrale

Un hôpital

DESCRIBING YOUR LOCAL AREA

Les bâtiments modernes/anciens – *Modern/Old buildings*

Une ville belle/laide – *A beautiful/ugly town*

Historique – *Historical*

Animé/Animée – *Lively*

Bruyant/Bruyante – *Loud*

Tranquille – *Quiet/Peaceful*

Sympatique – *Friendly*

Impersonnel – *Impersonal*

1.

J'adore ma ville. C'est un endroit urbain, donc il y a beaucoup de choses à faire, mais ce n'est pas trop bruyant. Ici c'est un quartier historique, et il y a plusieurs musées et galeries, donc c'est possible de passer la journée à se cultiver. Aussi, si on veut, on peut s'évader à la campagne très facilement par le train ; il y a un parc national à 12km seulement du centre-ville. En plus, nous avons l'internet à haut débit !

2.

Je n'aime pas vraiment mon village. Ici, je m'amuse bien, car ma maison est située près de celles de mes copains. Néanmoins, il n'y a pas grand-chose à faire. Il n'y a pas de cinéma, et très peu de commerces, donc on doit passer le temps comme on peut. Je ne suis pas encore en âge d'apprendre à conduire, donc je suis bloqué chez moi la plupart de temps.

3.

> Je déteste la vie dans ma ville. Ma famille a déménagé récemment, donc je n'ai pas d'amis à proximité. J'y suis habitué, mais je n'aime pas la ville elle-même –elle est bruyante, elle est salle, et les espaces verts me manquent.

Match the above opinions to their correct translations below by writing 1, 2 or 3 in the corresponding boxes:

I love my town. It's an urban area, so there are lots of things to do, but it is not too noisy. It's historic here, and with several museums and galleries, so it's possible to spend the day absorbing culture. Also, if you want, you can escape to the country very easily by train; there's a national park only 12km away from the town centre. In addition, we have high Internet speeds!

I hate life in my town. My family recently moved, so I don't have any friends close to me. I'm used to it, but I don't like the town itself. It's noisy, it's dirty, and I miss green spaces.

I don't really care for my village. I can enjoy myself here, as my house is nearby to my friends'. Nevertheless, there is not much to do. There's no cinema, very few shops, so you have to pass the time any way you can. I am not yet old enough to learn to drive, so I'm stuck at home most of the time.

Problems in town

Now, let's look at some more specific issues that people may have with their local area:

Le chômage	*Unemployment*
La pauvreté	*Poverty*
Le problème des sans-abris	*Homelessness*
Un manque d'emplois	*A lack of jobs*
Les réductions des aides financières	*Funding cuts*
Des comportements antisociaux	*Antisocial behaviour*
Le vandalisme	*Vandalism*

La banlieue

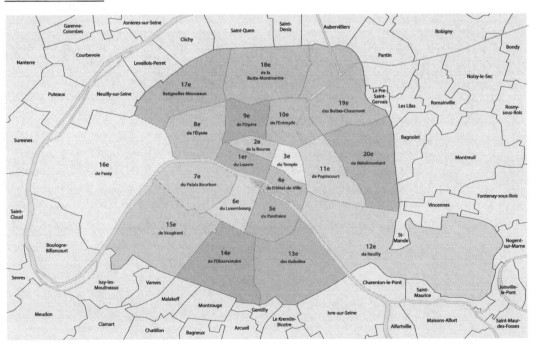

The above map shows the 20 *arrondissements* of Paris, the most exclusive of which are in the centre. The '*1er arrondissement*' contains the Louvre, Les Halles, and the Palais Royale. The areas in white encircling the city are the suburbs, or *banlieues* of Paris.

These are mostly residential, tend to be more multicultural, and are often painted in a bad light by conservative French media, due to a chequered history with the law. However, many believe any distrust of police comes from widespread institutionalised racism, as depicted in the 1995 film *La Haine* (Hatred), the plot of which revolves around police brutality geared towards migrants and their children following unrest, and the willingness of the French government to turn a blind eye to the huge social and financial disparity surrounding their capital.

Although the film is over 20 years old, many hold the opinion that the issues raised by it are today as relevant as ever, as the same problems remain in French society. In the context of the modern world, it could even be argued that this already sensitive situation has and will continue to deteriorate.

La diabolisation des jeunes de banlieue – *The demonisation of surburban youth*

La discrimination raciale – *Racial discrimination*

Un cercle vicieux – *A vicious circle*

Le refus de mettre en place des programmes de formation – *The unwillingness to put any training schemes in place*

Le rejet d'un candidat fondé sur leur adresse – *The rejection of job applicants based on their address*

PRACTICE EXAM QUESTION

Charity

Read the following conversation between these British students who are discussing their attitudes towards poverty and charity. Answer the questions below by circling **TRUE, FALSE or NOT MENTIONED**.

Molly : Le chômage et l'inégalité sociale sont deux des questions les plus pertinentes de nos jours. Il n'y a pas de solution parfaite, mais nous pouvons tous contribuer à améliorer la société. En premier lieu, il faut faire pression sur le gouvernement pour qu'il fournisser des fonds, et ensuite, comme communauté, il faut apporter des contributions personnelles.

Connor : Je crois que le problème de la misère est un scandale national. Je ne suis pas satisfait d'un statu quo dans lequel tellement de gens sont ignorés, et laissés pour morts. Je donne beaucoup d'argent à une grande variété d'organisations caritatives, mais c'est la responsabilité du gouvernement d'effectuer un changement réel, en changeant le système dans son intégralité.

Fareed : Selon moi, les sans-abri n'ont qu'à s'en prendre. Notre système de protection sociale est efficace, et il y a de nombreux régimes en place pour les aider. De plus, je pense qu'il devrait être illégal de mendier dans la rue, parce que les SDF sont tous des alcooliques et toxicomanes. Franchement, je crois que ces gens ont besoin de faire un effort pour trouver du travail.

Grace : Pour moi, les gens sont trop disposés à ignorer la pauvreté. Pour la majorité de la population, voire un SDF n'est rien d'autre qu'un inconvénient. La réaction publique s'est déplacée du choc vers l'indifférence. Il ne faut pas oublier que les sans-abris sont des êtres humains – ils ont besoin de notre aide et ils méritent notre attention.

Question 1

Molly believes that unemployment and social inequality are very important issues.

TRUE	FALSE	NOT MENTIONED

Question 2

Connor blames homelessness and poverty on the government.

TRUE	FALSE	NOT MENTIONED

Question 3

Fareed thinks the welfare system is not up to scratch.

TRUE	FALSE	NOT MENTIONED

Question 4

Grace thinks people have become desensitised to seeing homeless people.

TRUE	FALSE	NOT MENTIONED

Question 5

Molly thinks that the government should prioritise apprenticehip schemes.

TRUE	FALSE	NOT MENTIONED

Question 6

Connor wants to see government ministers punished for their inaction.

TRUE	FALSE	NOT MENTIONED

Question 7

Fareed thinks that it is possible to be hardworking and homeless.

TRUE	FALSE	NOT MENTIONED

Question 8

Grace believes homelessness is an issue which deserves our attention.

TRUE	FALSE	NOT MENTIONED

(Answers are provided at the back of the book).

THE ENVIRONMENT

The topic of the environment is an absolute favourite of examiners. It is all but guaranteed that you will have to deal with this topic in your listening and reading exams, so make sure you revise these next few pages thoroughly. Teachers also enjoy setting writing and speaking topics around this subject, so get practicing! Let's begin with some vocabulary:

Les ressources naturelles	*Natural resources*
La pollution	*Pollution*
Les usines	*Factories*
Le réchauffement de la planète	*Global warming*
L'effet de serre	*The greenhouse effect*
La fonte de la banquise	*The melting of the icecaps*
La disparition des espèces	*The extinction of species*
La consommation excessive	*Excessive consumption*
Les déchets	*Waste/Rubbish*
Gaspiller	*To waste*
La déforestation	*Deforestation*

More key terms :

Les gaz d'échappement – *Exhaust fumes*

La circulation - *Traffic*

Les embouteillages – *Traffic jams*

L'heure de pointe – *Rush hour*

La pluie acide – *Acid rain*

La sauvegarde de la nature – *Nature conservation*

Économiser – *To conserve*

Recycler/Faire du recyclage – *To recycle*

Réutiliser – *To reuse*

Trier les déchets (selon les catégories) – *To sort waste (into categories)*

Une contravention – *A fine*

Les transports en commun – *Public transport*

Faire du vélo – *Riding a bike*

Les pistes cyclables – *Cycle lanes*

Un débat

En ce qui me concerne, c'est honteux que le gouvernement n'ait rien fait pour combattre le réchauffement de la planète. La pollution est à son plus haut niveau, et personne ne veut agir. Je suis enragé.

Selon moi, c'est trop facile de dire que c'est la faute du gouvernement. C'est la responsabilité de chacun. Les petits gestes que tout le monde peut faire vont changer les choses.

Je ne suis pas d'accord. Les choses comme le recyclage sont devenues la norme pour la grande majorité du public, et les recherches effectuées par les scientifiques montrent une détérioration constante.

Je ne comprends pas ce que tu veux que le gouvernement fasse. Il a encouragé les gens à être conscients et modifier leurs routines quotidiennes. En plus, les centres de recyclage ont été construits partout !

Le recyclage est bon, mais le vrai problème réside dans les émissions massives causées par les fumées d'usines. Il faut récompenser les entreprises 'vertes' et imposer les centrales à charbon.

EDUCATION
AND
WORK

Vocabulary:

Les devoirs	Homework
Les notes	Grades
L'horaire	Timetable
La récréation	Break
La pause déjeuner	Lunch break
Un cours obligatoire	A compulsory course
Un cours facultatif	An optional course
Les règles	The rules

My favourite lessons:

Ce que je trouve intéressant, c'est la biologie
What I find interesting is biology

Étudier la musique, c'est mon truc
Studying music is my thing

Les mathématiques, ça me paraît logique
Maths is logical to me

J'aime beaucoup d'étudier les grands écrivains du passé en anglais
I love studying the great authors of the past in English

Je suis fort(e) en sport, donc j'adore les cours d'éducation physique
I am good at sport, so I love PE

My least favourite lessons:

Je ne peux pas comprendre la chimie
I can't understand chemistry

Je me sens forcé(e) d'apprendre des langues étrangères modernes
I feel obliged to learn modern foreign languages

C'est une lutte quotidienne pour me concentrer sur l'informatique
It's a daily battle fore me to concentrate on ICT

Je n'ai aucun talent artistique
I have no artistic talent

L'éducation religieuse ne m'excite guère
Religious Education doesn't excite me very much at all

Post-School Plans

Après le lycée – *After school*

J'ai envie de... - *I want to...*

J'aimerais avoir de bons résultats aux examens – *I would like to get good exam results*

J'espère décrocher un bon emploi – *I hope to land a good job*

J'ai l'intention d'aller à l'université – *I would like to go to university*

Faire un apprentissage – *Doing an apprenticeship*

Faire une licence – *Doing a degree*

Faire un programme de formation – *Undertaking a training scheme*

PRACTICE EXAM QUESTION

School life and the future

Read the conversation between these British students who are discussing education and their post-school lives. Answer the questions below **in English**.

Robert: Mes études préférées ont toujours été les sciences et les mathématiques. Depuis l'école primaire, j'ai réussi et toujours obtenu de bons résultats. Maintenant, je suis en train de postuler à des programmes de stage dans l'industrie. Donc, je prévois de faire une licence en ingénierie à une université prestigieuse, et de décrocher un emploi dans une entreprise renommée.

Tara: Au collège, je ne m'intéressais pas aux matières académiques traditionnelles. Au lieu de cela, je me concentrais totalement sur la musique ; j'adore composer, et je joue plusieurs instruments, dont mon préféré est la clarinette. A cause de cela, j'avais toujours du mal à avoir de bonnes notes. Alors, je serai une musicienne célèbre dans le monde entier !

Ryan: J'ai dix-sept ans, et je suis en terminale au lycée. Je me considère comme un étudiant moyen, qui se sent bien en classe, mais, j'ai une panne d'inspiration lorsqu'il s'agit de mon futur métier. En ce moment, je ne veux que sortir avec mes amis et ne pas penser à l'avenir.

Question 1

What does Robert say about his marks at school?

Question 2

What did Tara choose to prioritise ahead of her studies?

Question 3

What does Ryan say about his plans for a future profession?

Question 4

What does Robert want to do after he gets a degree in Engineering?

Question 5

What is Tara's aspiration?

Question 6

What are Ryan's feelings towards thinking about the future in general?

(Answers are provided at the end of the book).

GRAMMAR

Of course, all the vocab knowledge and insightful opinions in the world mean very little if they cannot be conveyed correctly and with grammatical accuracy. A range of verb tenses and grammatical features have been demonstrated throughout this guide. This section will provide you with easy, quick and simple explanations, on the fundamental elements on grammar required for GCSE French.

Nouns

A noun constitutes something that is an **object, a living thing, a person,** as well as something that is a **general concept.**

Examples:

Le kangarou (masc.) -	The kangaroo	*Un kangarou* – A kangaroo
La calculatrice (fem.) -	The calculator	*Une calculatrice* – A calculator
Le/La scientifique (m/f.) -	The scientist	*Un/Une scientifique* – A scientist
Le sexisme -	Sexism	

All nouns in French have gender – they are either masculine or feminine. Gender determines which of the definite and indefinite articles to use when referring to a certain noun, i.e. when to use *le/la* for 'the', or *un/une* for 'a'.

Nouns can either be **singular** or **plural**.

As in English, the most common way to make a noun plural is to add an 's':

Examples:

Un portable ⟶ *Deux portables*

One laptop   Two laptops

Une fleur	⟶	*Deux fleurs*
One flower		Two flowers

However, as you know, the plural forms of some nouns are irregular:

Nouns ending with 's', 'x' and 'z' are not made plural by adding an 's'; the plural forms of these nouns are identical to their singular forms:

Examples:

Un mois	⟶	*Deux mois*
One month		Two months

Un choix	⟶	*Deux choix*
One choice		Two choices

Un gaz	⟶	*Deux gaz*
One gas		Two gases

Nouns ending with 'au', 'eau', 'eu', and some nouns ending in 'ou', are not made plural by adding 's', but by adding 'x':

Examples:

Un joyau	⟶	*Deux joyaux*
One jewel		Two jewels

Un bureau	⟶	*Deux bureaux*
One office		Two offices

Un jeu   ⟶   *Deux jeux*

One game   Two games

Un chou   ⟶   *Deux choux*

One cabbage   Two cabbages

Nouns ending with '*ail*' and '*al*' are made plural by adding 'aux':

Examples:

Un travail   ⟶   *Deux travaux*

One job   Two jobs

Un animal   ⟶   *Deux animaux*

One animal   Two animals

Some nouns' plural forms are totally irregular:

Examples:

Un œil   ⟶   *Deux yeux*

One eye   Two eyes

Un Monsieur   ⟶   *Deux Messieurs*

One gentleman   Two gentlemen

Une Madame   ⟶   *Deux Mesdames*

One lady   Two ladies

Gender also plays a part when using the prepositions 'à' and 'de' before nouns.

<u>à</u>

à + le = au   ⟶   *au lycée*

at school/in school/to school

à + la = à la   ⟶   *à la boulangerie*

at the bakery/in the bakery/to the bakery

à + l' = à l'   ⟶   *à l'hôpital*

at the hospital/in the hospital/to the hospital

à + les = aux   ⟶   *aux banlieues*

in the suburbs/to the suburbs

<u>de</u>

de + le = du   ⟶   *du médecin*

of the doctor/the doctor's (possession)

de + la = de la   ⟶   *de la famille*

of the family/the family's (possession)

de + l' = de l'   ⟶   *de l'entreprise*

of the business/the business' (possession)

de + les = des   ⟶   *des victims*

of the victims/the victims' (possession)

Adjectives

Adjectives are used to describe nouns and pronouns, and in order to be used accurately, they need to agree according to gender.

> **Most adjectives change to agree by adding an 'e' to (its masculine form) when used to describe a feminine noun, an 's' when used to describe a masculine noun in the plural form, and 'es' when used to describe a feminine noun in the plural:**

Examples:

Masc sing- *Un costume élégant* ➤ A smart suit

Fem sing- *Une chemise élégante* ➤ A smart shirt

Masc pl- *Deux costumes élégants* ➤ Two smart suits

Fem pl- *Deux chemises élegantes* ➤ Two smart shirts

> **However, adjectives whose singular masculine forms end in 's' do not require another 's' to be added when referring to a masculine noun in the plural. Similarly, adjectives whose singular masculine forms end in 'e', do not require another 'e' to be added when referring to a feminine noun in the singular.**

Examples:

Masc sing- *Un serveur français* ➤ A French waiter

Fem sing- *Une recette française* ➤ A French recipe

Masc pl- *Deux serveurs français* ➤ Two French waiters

Fem pl- *Deux recettes françaises* ➤ Two French recipes

> There are also many irregular adjectives that not agree in this way.
>
> Firstly, as with nouns ending with '*al*', the vast majority of adjectives whose singular masculine forms end with '*al*', use the ending '*aux*' to describe plural masculine nouns. Adjectives ending with '*al*´ being used to describe feminine nouns, both in the singular and plural, are formed in the regular way, by adding '*e*' and '*es*'.

Examples:

Masc sing-	*Un aperçu général*	⟶	A general overview
Fem sing-	*Une demande générale*	⟶	A general inquiry
Masc pl-	*Deux aperçus généraux*	⟶	Two general overviews
Fem pl-	*Deux demandes générales*	⟶	Two general inquiries

> Adjectives whose singular masculine forms end with '*el*', '*et*', '*eil*', '*ien*', '*il*' and '*n*' change regularly to agree with forms of nouns except the feminine, in which case the final consonant is doubled as well as an '*e*' being added.

Examples:

Masc sing-	*Un repas traditionnel*	⟶	A traditional meal
Fem sing-	*Une boisson traditionnelle*	⟶	A traditional drink
Masc pl-	*Deux repas traditionnels*	⟶	Two traditional meals
Fem pl-	*Deux boissons traditionnelles*	⟶	Two traditional drinks

Masc sing-	*Un homme gentil*	⟶	A kind man
Fem sing-	*Une femme gentille*	⟶	A kind woman
Masc pl-	*Deux hommes gentils*	⟶	Two kind men
Fem pl-	*Deux femmes gentilles*	⟶	Two kind women

> **Adjectives whose singular masculine forms end with '*f*' change this ending to '*ve*' and '*ves*' when used in the feminine forms.**

Examples:

Masc sing-	*Un taureau agressif*	➤	An agressive bull
Fem sing-	*Une vache agressive*	➤	An agressive cow
Masc pl-	*Deux taureau agressifs*	➤	Two agressive bulls
Fem pl-	*Deux vaches agressives*	➤	Two agressive cows

> **Adjectives whose singular masculine form ends with '*er*' change this ending to '*ère*' and '*ères*' when used in the feminine forms.**

Examples:

Masc sing-	*Un smartphone cher*	➤	An expensive smartphone
Fem sing-	*Une voiture chère*	➤	An expensive car
Masc pl-	*Deux smartphones chers*	➤	Two expensive smartphones
Fem pl-	*Deux voitures chères*	➤	Two expensive cars

> **The vast majority of adjectives whose singular masculine forms end with '*x*' do not change when referring to masculine nouns in the plural, and this ending changes to '*se*' and '*ses*' in the feminine forms.**

Examples:

Masc sing-	*Un lieu dangereux*	➤	A dangerous place
Fem sing-	*Une zone dangereuse*	➤	A dangerous area
Masc pl-	*Deux lieus dangereux*	➤	Two dangerous places
Fem pl-	*Deux zones dangereuses*	➤	Two dangerous areas

> Adjectives whose singular masculine form ends with '*c*' change this ending to '*che*' and '*ches*' when used in the feminine forms.

Examples:

Masc sing-	*Un point blanc*	⟶	A white dot
Fem sing-	*Une bande blanche*	⟶	A white stripe
Masc pl-	*Deux points blancs*	⟶	Two white dots
Fem pl-	*Deux bandes blanches*	⟶	Two white stripes

As you will know, in French the vast majority of adjectives are placed **after** the noun they are describing. However, there is a group of very common adjectives that are more often than not placed **before** the noun. It will be extremely helpful to learn these, as it is a very common mistake to assume that adjectives always appear after the noun they refer to, as you will have been taught the 'adjectives come after nouns' rule from Year 7.

Here are the common adjectives that come before the noun:

Bon/Bonne	***Mauvais/Mauvaise***
Good	Bad
Petit/Petite	***Grand/Grande***
Small	Big
Jeune	
Young	***Vieux/Vielle***
Nouveau/Nouvelle	Old
New	

Joli/Jolie	*Méchant/Méchante*
Kind/Nice	Mean
Court/Courte	*Long/Longe*
Short	Long
Meilleur/Meilleure	*Pire*
Better	Worse

Examples:

- *Le **petit** chat a traversé la rue* ⟶ The little cat crossed the road
- *J'habite une **jolie** ville* ⟶ I live in a nice town
- *Obtenir un **meilleur** accord* ⟶ To get a better deal

Adverbs

Generally, adverbs can be defined as verbs descriptors, or as being like adjectives for verbs. They are also used to qualify adjectives themselves, as well as other adverbs.

In French, adverbs form themselves in a very similar way as they do in English, in two common ways:

1. Derived from adjectives; by adding '*ment*' to the feminine form (similar to adding '*ly*' to an adjective in English – e.g. 'slow' becomes 'slowly')

   Examples:

   - *Le couple se promène **lentement*** ⟶ The couple walks **slowly**

     (Feminine form of 'slow' is '*lente*' + '*ment*' = '*lentement*')

   - *Il faut le changer **radicalement*** ⟶ It needs to change **radically**

(Feminine form of 'radical' is 'radicale' + 'ment' = 'radicalement')

2. As distinct words of their own, not derived from adjectives. Again, this is very similar to how they appear in English.

Examples:

Beaucoup	*Assez*
A lot	Enough
Petit/Petite	*Grand/Grande*
Small	Big
Souvent	*Déjà*
Often	Already
Ici	*Là*
Kind/Nice	Mean

Verbs

The present tense

Of course, the present tense is used commonly:

* To describe actions occurring at that present time (e.g. The man is dancing)

* To describe actions that happen regularly (e.g. I swim every week)

* To describe actions that are about to happen in the immediate future (e.g. We're going to order a pizza in two hours)

* To describe things that are generally observable (e.g. Bulbasaur is a poor choice of starter)

In French, most verbs follow one of the three set rules of conjugation. You will know which of these sets of rules is correct by looking at whether a verb ends in '**er**', '**ir**' or '**re**'. Here are the set rules for conjugating each type of verb in the present tense:

Regular 'ER' verb endings

To demonstrate, the regular verb '*jouer*' will be conjugated.

Jouer – To play

I	*Je*	*jou**e***	(I play)
You (sing.)	*Tu*	*jou**es***	(You play)
He/She/It	*Il/Elle*	*jou**e***	(He/She/It plays)
We	*Nous*	*jou**ons***	(We play)
You (pl.)	*Vous*	*jou**ez***	(You play)
They	*Ils*	*jou**ent***	(They play)

Regular 'IR' verb endings

To demonstrate, the regular verb '*finir*' will be conjugated.

Finir – To finish

I	*Je*	*fin**is***	(I finish)
You (sing.)	*Tu*	*fin**is***	(You finish)
He/She/It	*Il/Elle*	*fin**it***	(He/She/It finishes)
We	*Nous*	*fin**issons***	(We finish)
You (pl.)	*Vous*	*fin**issez***	(You finish)
They	*Ils*	*fin**issent***	(They finish)

Regular '*RE*' verb endings

To demonstrate, the regular verb '*vendre*' will be conjugated.

Vendre – To sell

I	**Je**	*vend***s**	(I sell)
You (sing.)	**Tu**	*vend***s**	(You sell)
He/She/It	**Il/Elle**	*vend*	(He/She/It sells)
We	**Nous**	*vend***ons**	(We sell)
You (pl.)	**Vous**	*vend***ez**	(You sell)
They	**Ils**	*vend***ent**	(They sell)

The perfect tense

On the surface, the perfect tense in French seems to be the equivalent of the perfect tense in English, i.e. to explain what has happened, rather than simply 'what happened'. But, although this is literally the case, in practice the French perfect is used commonly to explain events that have happened, as the simple past tense is used in English.

The French perfect is formed using an **auxiliary verb** and a **past participle**, where the auxiliary verb is the one that is conjugated, and the past participle remains unchanged. For the vast majority of verbs, the auxiliary is the verb '*avoir*'. For example, the phrase 'I played' in English will be '*j'ai joué*', with '*ai*' literally translating to 'have' and '*joué* (the past participle) to 'played'. But, in practice, '*j'ai joué*' means 'I played'.

Regular '*ER*' verb endings

To demonstrate, the regular verb '*jouer*' will be conjugated.

Jouer – To play

I	J'	ai	joué	(I played)
You (sing.)	Tu	as	joué	(You played)
He/She/It	Il/Elle	a	joué	(He/She/It played)
We	Nous	avons	joué	(We played)
You (pl.)	Vous	avez	joué	(You played)
They	Ils	ont	joué	(They played)

Regular 'IR' verb endings

To demonstrate, the regular verb 'finir' will be conjugated.

Finir – To finish

I	J'	ai	fini	(I finished)
You (sing.)	Tu	as	fini	(You finished)
He/She/It	Il/Elle	a	fini	(He/She/It finished)
We	Nous	avons	fini	(We finished)
You (pl.)	Vous	avez	fini	(You finished)
They	Ils	ont	fini	(They finished)

Regular 'RE' verb endings

To demonstrate, the regular verb 'vendre' will be conjugated.

Vendre – To sell

I	*J'*	**ai**	*vend**u***	(I sold)
You (sing.)	*Tu*	**as**	*vend**u***	(You sold)
He/She/It	*Il/Elle*	**a**	*vend**u***	(He/She/It sold)
We	*Nous*	**avons**	*vend**u***	(We sold)
You (pl.)	*Vous*	**avez**	*vend**u***	(You sold)
They	*Ils*	**ont**	*vend**u***	(They sold)

So, as mentioned before, the vast majority of verbs form the perfect tense (and other compound tenses) with '*avoir*' as their auxiliary. However, there are 14 verbs that are constructed using '*être*', such as '*arriver*'. This means that 'I arrived' translates to '*Je suis arrivé(e)*'. Note that depending on whether the subject of the verb is feminine or plural, then the past participle has to agree by adding an extra 'e', 's', or 'es' accordingly. I.e. if the verb is referring to someone who is male, a group, someone who is female, or a group of women only, agreements have to be made.

Knowing this is a major key in your French study, as some of these tricky *être*-taking, agreement-needing verbs are some of the most important and commonly occurring of all. Here are the 14 '*être*' verbs, which you can remember by calling them the 'MRS VAN-DER-TRAMP' verbs, as they begin with the letters of this fictional lady's name. (Agreements have been marked in bold – adding an '**e**' is required when referring to the feminine in the singular, an '**s**' is used when referring to the masculine / the masculine and feminine in the plural, and '**es**' is used when referring to the feminine in the plural.

MONTER	➤	*Je suis monté/montée*	**(I climbed/went up)**
RESTER	➤	*Tu es resté/restée*	**(You stayed)**
SORTIR	➤	*Il est sorti/Elle a sortie*	**(He/She went out)**

VENIR → *Nous sommes venus/venues*   **(We came)**

ALLER → *Vous êtes allé/allée/allés/allées*   **(You went)**

NAÎTRE → *Ils sont nés/nées*   **(They were born)**

DESCENDRE → *Je suis descendu/descendue*   **(I descended)**

ENTRER → *Tu es entré/entrée*   **(You entered)**

RENTRER → *Il est rentré/Elle est rentrée*   **(He/She returned)**

TOMBER → *Nous sommes tombés/tombées*   **(We fell)**

RETOURNER → *Vous êtes retourné/retournée /retournés/retournées*   **(You returned)**

ARRIVER → *Ils sont arrivés/arrives*   **(They arrived)**

MOURIR → *Je suis mort/morte*   **(I died)**

PARTIR → *Tu est parti/partie*   **(You left)**

The imperfect tense

Like the perfect tense, the imperfect tense is used to refer to events that have happened in the past. The distinction between the tenses lies in whether the action has a clear start and end time, or if the action was completed. If it is not known or ambiguous, the action is incomplete, or 'imperfect'.

The main uses of the imperfect tense are:

- To describe past states and situations (e.g. During Shakespeare's time, acting was an exclusively male profession.)

- To describe what used to happen/recurring events that took place in the past (e.g. I used to work in a bank in Maidstone.)

Regular '*ER*' verb endings

To demonstrate, the regular verb '*jouer*' will be conjugated.

Jouer – To play

I	**Je**	*jou**ais***
You (sing.)	**Tu**	*jou**ais***
He/She/It	**Il/Elle**	*jou**ait***
We	**Nous**	*jou**ions***
You (pl.)	**Vous**	*jou**iez***
They	**Ils**	*jou**aient***

Regular '*IR*' verb endings

To demonstrate, the regular verb '*finir*' will be conjugated.

Finir – To finish

I	**Je**	*fin**issais***
You (sing.)	**Tu**	*fin**issais***
He/She/It	**Il/Elle**	*fin**issait***
We	**Nous**	*fin**issions***
You (pl.)	**Vous**	*fin**issiez***
They	**Ils**	*fin**issaient***

Regular 'RE' verb endings

To demonstrate, the regular verb 'vendre' will be conjugated.

Vendre – To sell

I	Je	vendais
You (sing.)	Tu	vendais
He/She/It	Il/Elle	vendait
We	Nous	vendions
You (pl.)	Vous	vendiez
They	Ils	vendaient

Verbs which most commonly used in the imperfect are '**avoir**', '**être**' and '**faire**'. Of course, these are irregular, but ones that are absolutely vital (as you know). So, here are a few examples of phrases in the imperfect that make use of these verbs.

Quand **j'étais** petit, je jouais très bien du piano. ⟶

When I was little, I played the piano very well.

Pendant les années 1990, les gens **avaient** de meilleures chances de s'acheter une maison. ⟶

During the 90s, people had a better chance of buying a house.

Il faisait beau le jour de notre mariage. ⟶

The weather was good on the day of our marriage.

The future

As in English, the French future tense modifies verbs in two ways – one for saying **what will happen** (the future tense), and one for saying **what is going to happen** (the immediate future). The difference between the two languages appears when saying **what will happen**, as in French, verb endings are used to express this idea, rather than a word equivalent to 'will' in this instance. But, the verb 'to go' ('*aller*') plus an infinitive is similarly used when saying **what is going to happen** in French.

<u>The future tense</u>

Regular '*ER*' verb endings

To demonstrate, the regular verb '*jouer*' will be conjugated.

Jouer – To play

I	*Je*	*jou**erai***	(I will play)
You (sing.)	*Tu*	*jou**eras***	(You will play)
He/She/It	*Il/Elle*	*jou**era***	(He/She/It will play)
We	*Nous*	*jou**erons***	(We will play)
You (pl.)	*Vous*	*jou**erez***	(You will play)
They	*Ils*	*jou**eront***	(They will play)

Regular '*IR*' verb endings

To demonstrate, the regular verb '*finir*' will be conjugated.

Finir – To finish

I	*Je*	*fin**irai***	(I will finish)
You (sing.)	*Tu*	*fin**iras***	(You will finish)
He/She/It	*Il/Elle*	*fin**ira***	(He/She/It will finish)
We	*Nous*	*fin**irons***	(We will finish)
You (pl.)	*Vous*	*fin**irez***	(You will finish)
They	*Ils*	*fin**iront***	(They will finish)

Regular '*RE*' verb endings

To demonstrate, the regular verb '*vendre*' will be conjugated.

Vendre – To sell

I	*Je*	*vend**rai***	(I will sell)
You (sing.)	*Tu*	*vend**ras***	(You will sell)
He/She/It	*Il/Elle*	*vend**ra***	(He/She/It will sell)
We	*Nous*	*vend**rons***	(We will sell)
You (pl.)	*Vous*	*vend**rez***	(You will sell)
They	*Ils*	*vend**ront***	(They will sell)

The immediate future

Regular '*ER*' verb endings

To demonstrate, the regular verb '*jouer*' will be conjugated.

Jouer – To play

I	Je	**vais**	jouer
You (sing.)	Tu	**vas**	jouer
He/She/It	Il/Elle	**va**	jouer
We	Nous	**allons**	jouer
You (pl.)	Vous	**allez**	jouer
They	Ils	**vont**	jouer

Regular 'IR' verb endings

To demonstrate, the regular verb '*finir*' will be conjugated.

Finir – To finish

I	Je	**vais**	finir
You (sing.)	Tu	**vas**	finir
He/She/It	Il/Elle	**va**	finir
We	Nous	**allons**	finir
You (pl.)	Vous	**allez**	finir
They	Ils	**vont**	finir

Regular 'RE' verb endings

To demonstrate, the regular verb '*vendre*' will be conjugated.

Vendre – To sell

I	*Je*	**vais**	*vendre*
You (sing.)	*Tu*	**vas**	*vendre*
He/She/It	*Il/Elle*	**va**	*vendre*
We	*Nous*	**allons**	*vendre*
You (pl.)	*Vous*	**allez**	*vendre*
They	*Ils*	**vont**	*vendre*

The conditional tense

The conditional in French is just as commonly used as in English and can most simply be defined as the tense that expresses what 'would happen'. For example – 'If Man City signed Lionel Messi, **they would win** the Champions League.' It can also be used when telling someone to do something, or when making a request. For example – '**Could you** stop poking me on Facebook, please?' or '**I'd like** a pineapple juice'.

Regular '*ER*' verb endings

To demonstrate, the regular verb '*jouer*' will be conjugated.

Jouer – To play

I	**Je**	*jou**erais***	(I would play)
You (sing.)	**Tu**	*jou**erais***	(You would play)
He/She/It	**Il/Elle**	*jou**erait***	(He/She/It would play)
We	**Nous**	*jou**erions***	(We would play)
You (pl.)	**Vous**	*jou**eriez***	(You would play)
They	**Ils**	*jou**eraient***	(They would play)

Regular 'IR' verb endings

To demonstrate, the regular verb '*finir*' will be conjugated.

Finir – To finish

I	*Je*	*fin**irai***	(I would finish)
You (sing.)	*Tu*	*fin**iras***	(You would finish)
He/She/It	*Il/Elle*	*fin**ira***	(He/She/It would finish)
We	*Nous*	*fin**irons***	(We would finish)
You (pl.)	*Vous*	*fin**irez***	(You would finish)
They	*Ils*	*fin**iront***	(They would finish)

Regular 'RE' verb endings

To demonstrate, the regular verb '*vendre*' will be conjugated.

Vendre – To sell

I	*Je*	*vend**rai***	(I would sell)
You (sing.)	*Tu*	*vend**ras***	(You would sell)
He/She/It	*Il/Elle*	*vend**ra***	(He/She/It would sell)
We	*Nous*	*vend**rons***	(We would sell)
You (pl.)	*Vous*	*vend**rez***	(You would sell)
They	*Ils*	*vend**ront***	(They would sell)

Prepositions

Prepositions are used to link many types of words in order to indicate when, where and why something happens, by providing extra information that a sentence without a preposition would provide.

Example:

Simple sentence with **NO** preposition:

José was crying.

Sentence **WITH** preposition:

*José was crying **about** his bank balance **underneath** his bed.*

So, the preposition in this case 'about', told us why José had reason to cry, and 'underneath' told us where he was doing it.

See below for explanations and examples for the two most commonly occurring prepositions in French, '*à*' and '*de*'.

À vs De

An extremely common struggle foreigners have while studying French is centred around knowing when to use 'a' or 'de', and dealing with the multiple ways sentences containing these prepositions can be translated. However, there are some general rules which more often than not prove to be true.

À

- Usually means 'to' – For example: *Il va à Londres* – He's going to London **(Not when 'to' is referring to a feminine country – in which case use '*en*')**

- Can mean 'in' – For example: *Elle travaille à Cardiff* – She works in Cardiff **(Not when 'in' is referring to something being inside of something else – in which case use '*dans*')**

- Can mean 'at' – For example: *Je suis à collège* – I am at school

- There are some phrases that mean some verbs **must** be followed by '*à*' if used before nouns or infinitives. Some common phrases with this rule are:

  o *Acheter à (quelque part)* – To buy **from** (somewhere)

  o *Apprendre à (verb)* – To learn how to (verb)

  o *Demander à (quelq'un)* – To ask (someone)

  o *Dire à (quelqu'un)* – To tell (someone)

  o *Encourager à (verb)* – To encourage to (verb)

  o *S'intéresser à (verb)* – To be interested in (verb)

  o *Jouer à (quelque chose)* – To play (something)

  o *Parler à (quelqu'un)* – To talk **to** (someone)

  o *Penser à (quelque chose)* – To think about (something)

  o *Parler à (quelqu'un)* – To talk **to** (someone)

De

- Usually means 'of' – For example: *Une tasse de thé* – A cup of tea. Similarly, '*de*' is used to denote possession. For example: *La voiture de Josh* – Josh's car.

- Usually means 'from' – For example: *Je viens de Birkenhead* – I am from Birkenhead.

- Can mean 'about' – For example: *Un film de science-fiction* – A science-fiction film.

- There are some phrases that mean some verbs **must** be followed by '*de*' if used before nouns or infinitives. Some common phrases with this rule are:

  o *Avoir besoin **de** (quelque chose)* – To need (something)

  o *Avoir peur **de** (quelque chose)* – To fear (something)

o *Choisir **de** (quelque chose)* – To choose (something)

o *Décider **de** (verb)* – To decide to (verb)

o *Essayer **de** (verb)* – To try to (verb)

o *Rire **de** (quelque chose)* – To laugh at (something)

o *S'occuper **de** (quelque chose)* – To be busy with (something)

o *Venir **de** quelque chose (verb)* – To have just done something (verb)

ANSWERS

My timetable

1. 8:40 (am)
2. 1:30pm/13:30
3. 7am/7:00
4. Ashley
5. Stephen
6. Katie

Planning a party

1. A
2. C
3. A
4. C
5. B

My family life

1. She has no independence, and her parents are too strict
2. 3 – his father and two sisters
3. 0 – he is the eldest child
4. She didn't like it – she was sad
5. Because there would be boys there
6. He says he is not always the centre of attention
7. His mum simply needs the help
8. She viewed him as an intruder

Daily Routine

1. réveille
2. lève
3. rester
4. douche
5. brosse

6. habille
7. prends
8. quitter
9. aller
10. arrive
11. doit
12. a
13. rentrer
14. détend
15. regarder
16. faire
17. nettoyer
18. prépare
19. coucher
20. navigue
21. endors

Grasse Bretagne

1. The UK has the highest rate of obesity in Europe/24.9% of the British population is obese/50% could be obese by 2050

2. Our lives are increasingly sedentary + things that are bad for us are very easily accessible

3. We cannot continue down this road of irresponsibility

4. The government must crack down on binge drinking + raise taxes on tobacco

5. Getting enough sleep + managing stress well

6. Obesity is one of the worst health threats of our time, and we must take decisive action, lest we condemn ourselves to disaster

My hobbies

1. False – (Erik uses music to switch off and relax)

2. True

3. Not Mentioned

4. False – (Daniel thinks television is a waste of time)

5. True

6. False – (Harry doesn't say when he started skating, but mentions problems he had skating in public before the park was built)

7. True

8. True

The evolution of tourism

1. They are now as popular as each other

2. They are no longer going to Spain every year – rather choosing to discover new countries

3. Holidaymakers are making use of low-cost air travel – they fly to one city, tour Europe by train, and then fly home from a different airport.

4. Smartphone culture.

5. More and more short stays in cities are booked all year round.

6. British holidaymakers becoming more adventurous + travel costs going down + more readily available tourist information.

Benefits and Drawbacks of Social Media

Les bienfaits

Les réseaux sociaux sont excellents pour garder le contact avec tes proches.

On peut se connecter instantanément avec les copains pour planifier un événement.

C'est facile de partager les beaux moments de ta vie avec tes amis.

Avoir un profil Internet apprend aux jeunes à développer leur identité et trouver leur propre voix.

Des plateformes comme Facebook peuvent sensibiliser le public aux sujets importants.

Platforms like Facebook can raise public awareness about important subjects.

Having an internet profile teaches young people to develop their identities and find a distinct voice of their own

You can instantly connect with friends to plan an event.

It's easy to share your life's best moments with your friends.

Social networks are great for keeping in touch with friends and family.

Les risques

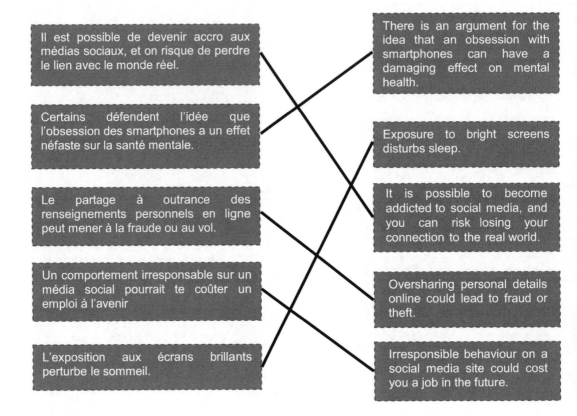

Il est possible de devenir accro aux médias sociaux, et on risque de perdre le lien avec le monde réel.

There is an argument for the idea that an obsession with smartphones can have a damaging effect on mental health.

Certains défendent l'idée que l'obsession des smartphones a un effet néfaste sur la santé mentale.

Exposure to bright screens disturbs sleep.

Le partage à outrance des renseignements personnels en ligne peut mener à la fraude ou au vol.

It is possible to become addicted to social media, and you can risk losing your connection to the real world.

Un comportement irresponsable sur un média social pourrait te coûter un emploi à l'avenir

Oversharing personal details online could lead to fraud or theft.

L'exposition aux écrans brillants perturbe le sommeil.

Irresponsible behaviour on a social media site could cost you a job in the future.

<u>Charity</u>

1. True

2. True

3. False – (Fareed thinks that the welfare system is efficient, and that there are many systems in place to help)

4. True

5. Not mentioned

6. Not mentioned

7. False – (Fareed thinks that homeless people need to put an effort into finding a job, and implies that this will solve their problems)

8. True

School life and the future

1. They have always been good
2. Music (composing and playing several instruments)
3. He has a lack of inspiration
4. Land a job at a top firm
5. To be a world famous musician
6. He does not want to think about it

Get Access To

FREE

Psychometric Tests

www.PsychometricTestsOnline.co.uk